D0836947

The College Completion Glass— Half-Full or Half-Empty?

The College Completion Glass— Half-Full or Half-Empty?

Exploring the Value of Postsecondary Education

Tiffany Beth Mfume

ROWMAN & LITTLEFIELD
Lanham • Boulder • New York • London

Published by Rowman & Littlefield
An imprint of The Rowman & Littlefield Publishing Group, Inc.
4501 Forbes Boulevard, Suite 200, Lanham, Maryland 20706
https://rowman.com

6 Tinworth Street, London SE11 5AL, United Kingdom

Copyright © 2019 by Tiffany Beth Mfume

All rights reserved. No part of this book may be reproduced in any form or by any electronic or mechanical means, including information storage and retrieval systems, without written permission from the publisher, except by a reviewer who may quote passages in a review.

British Library Cataloguing in Publication Information Available

Library of Congress Cataloging-in-Publication Data

Includes bibliographic references.
ISBN 9781475839593 (cloth : alk. paper)
ISBN 9781475839609 (pbk. : alk. paper)
ISBN 9781475839616 (Electronic)

♾ ™ The paper used in this publication meets the minimum requirements of American National Standard for Information Sciences Permanence of Paper for Printed Library Materials, ANSI/NISO Z39.48-1992.

Printed in the United States of America

Contents

Preface

This book is a follow-up to my 2016 book, *What Works at Historically Black Colleges and Universities (HBCUs): Nine Strategies for Increasing Retention and Graduation Rates.* While my first book represents the culmination of my professional career experience at my alma mater, Morgan State University, this second book really serves as my response to a growing culture of negativity toward postsecondary education. Concerns about student loan debt, the employment rate of college graduates, and the viability of institutions of higher learning leave many people asking, "Is a college degree really worth it?" Further, I've observed higher-education professionals being critical of ourselves when it comes to retention and graduation rates.

I attend about a dozen conferences and convenings per year, and it is not uncommon to explore deficit-style themes in reference to what is missing in higher education, what institutions are not doing well in higher education, and what changes need to be made to "save" higher education. Of course, higher-education professionals can do better by improving systems; educating students well; and preparing college graduates to take on the challenges of graduate school, career, entrepreneurship, volunteerism, and civic engagement. However, educators and critics of postsecondary education often dwell on the half-empty portion instead of the half-full portion of the college-completion glass.

More than half of all students at four-year postsecondary institutions actually graduate according to the stringent federal definition of *college graduation* thoroughly explained in chapter 1 of this book. I believe that a focus on what we've done well for the half of students who do finish on time can inform our efforts to enhance student success and increase college completion rates for the other half.

I continue to challenge federal guidelines for retention and graduation rates that exclude transfer students, mature students, part-time students, and students who begin college in terms other than fall. I question the value of performance-based funding models and other state policies that undermine student success and disadvantage institutions and colleges that serve minority and underserved populations.

I will always advocate for historically black colleges and universities; I am a proud product of a rich and broad HBCU educational experience. I continue to highlight our work at Morgan State University in this book and frame it in the context of current literature and research in higher education. I share with the readers of this book some of my personal stories to support my larger concepts. These stories represent my perceptions and recollections of the events that have influenced, affected, and shaped our success model at Morgan State University.

Beginning with the fall 2010 freshmen cohort, Morgan has achieved retention rates above 70 percent for seven consecutive years. As a result of grants from the Lumina Foundation, the Bill & Melinda Gates Foundation, and the Maryland Higher Education Commission, Morgan has invested in new technologies, including the Education Advisory Board's (EAB) Student Success Collaborative (SSC), Hobson's Starfish Retention Solutions, and Ellucian's Degree Works. These tools have assisted Morgan's Office of Student Success and Retention with strategic tracking and monitoring, auditing and degree planning, academic coaching and mentoring, course redesign, and predictive analytics.

Our intrusive, intentional student success initiatives have helped Morgan gain national recognition for our efforts, resulting in the 2017 Hobsons Education Advances Award for Student Success and Advisement, the Association of Public and Land-Grant Universities' (APLU) 2016 Turning Points Award, and the 2015 APLU Project Degree Completion Award for our outstanding efforts to increase retention rates and promote student success. Morgan State University is the only HBCU to ever have won these national awards.

This book serves as a foundational and encompassing document for the exploration of the value of postsecondary education. It can serve as a guide for colleges and universities in the nation to study, motivate, and inspire effective, data-driven strategies, best practices, and innovations; it is written to defend and champion the value of postsecondary education while promoting student success and ultimately stimulating the exchange of ideas.

Acknowledgments

I am grateful that I have been strongly encouraged by my family, my mentors, and my colleagues to write a second book. First and foremost, I truly thank my partner, my best friend, my mentor and the love of my life, my husband, Kweisi Mfume. Honey, your ongoing encouragement and never-ending support means the world to me; thank you for allowing me to go down this road again! I sincerely thank my parents, Betha and Lois McMillan, whom I credit with any and all of my professional and personal successes. I am blessed to be the progeny of an English professor and a mathematics professor who met and fell in love on the campus of Morgan State College in 1970.

I owe this second book project entirely to my younger sister and book-writing mentor, Dr. Angela McMillan Howell. When Angela published *Raised Up Down Yonder: Growing Up Black in Rural Alabama* in 2013, she set the standard in our family for academic rigor. Thank you, Angela, for your sound wisdom and great advice and for letting me know that I had a second book in me. I thank my youngest sister, Sally, my attorney, for her example of strength and courage. Sally, you are a strong, beautiful, young woman; you continue to demonstrate resilience and relentlessness in every aspect of your life! I thank my awesome brother, David; his lovely wife, Jen; and my adorable nephews, James McMillan and Elijah McMillan; my brother-in-law, Dr. Ricardo O. Howell; my wonderful niece (and goddaughter), Lily Isabella Howell; and my charming nephew, Levi Howell. I thank my three amazing sisters-in-law, Darlene, Lawana, and Michelle, and my husband's entire family, especially my fantastic grandchildren.

I have been blessed by a number of mentors who have encouraged me in different ways at different points in my professional career. I thank Dr. John Hudgins at Coppin State University for first opening my eyes to the correct interpretation of data during my graduate program in sociology, for helping me to look beyond the popular data points and examine the truth and reality behind the data, and for asking me every year when would I be writing my book. I thank Dr. Maurice Taylor for encouraging me to network with colleagues from across the country, step outside of the "HBCU box," and never neglect my own professional development.

I thank my supervisor of ten years, Dr. Kara M. Turner, vice president of Enrollment Management and Student Success (EMASS) at Morgan State University, for holding me to the highest of standards and expecting excellence from me at all times; you are a great leader! I thank both Dr. Earl S. Richardson and Dr. David Wilson, two great college presidents and lovers of Morgan State University. I thank my EMASS colleagues at Morgan, all under the supervision of Dr. Kara Turner: Ernest Brevard Jr., Dr. Brenda James, Adrienne Karasik, Keisha Campbell, Tanya Wilkerson, and Shonda Gray-Cain—"Teamwork still makes the dream work!" I sincerely thank my Office of Student Success and Retention (OSSR) staff at Morgan State University, the "A team" at MSU!

To God be the glory, great things He has done.

Chapter One

Graduation Rates 101

It is virtually impossible to find any book, white paper, article, report, or blog in the field of higher education without the words *persistence*, *progression*, *retention*, *graduation*, or *completion* appearing somewhere in the title, headline, thesis statement, byline, or text. Thanks to an increased emphasis on accountability, student outcomes, and data, colleges and universities are in a perpetual state of reporting out retention, persistence, and graduation rates, with detailed plans and strategies to increase college completion.

The national graduation rate of approximately 59 percent for all four-year institutions of all types suggests that more than half of all students who begin college at a four-year institution will earn a bachelor's degree in six years or less (Ginder, Kelly-Reid, & Mann, 2017). Over the last two decades, the aggregate 50/50 chance of graduating on time has left many experts in the field of higher education questioning their moral obligation to entering college students, so they have conducted self-studies to better understand attrition variables and organized programs and initiatives to improve college completion rates.

At the heart of this issue of low graduation rates, however, is the measurement and calculation of college graduation rates by the US Department of Education. The National Center for Education Statistics (NCES) counts graduation rates as the percentage of first-time, full-time freshmen in a cohort who begin at a college or university in the fall term and complete their degree in 6 years or 12 consecutive semesters or less at the same institution.

This definition is limiting for a number of reasons discussed in this book, and efforts to redefine the measurement for two-year and four-year institutions of higher learning are well underway, including the national campaign #countallstudents. Until such changes and redefinitions are enacted, the reality of mediocre graduation rates looms in postsecondary education.

But, is the college completion glass really half-empty as these data suggest? Is the country really wasting tax dollars and precious resources by throwing "bad money" behind "good money" to try to fix a fundamentally flawed system of higher education? Or, is the glass actually half-full? At least half of all students complete their degree at the same institution where they began their postsecondary education, but what about the success of the many transfer students, mature students, and part-time students who will eventually earn a bachelor's degree? Shouldn't their success matter?

This book argues that the value added of even one year of college is transformative. Although colleges and universities often are indicted when students don't complete college, what system is collecting data about the success of students who attended college but never completed a degree? So-called college dropouts such as Bill Gates, Steve Jobs, P. Diddy, and Mark Zuckerberg are just a few examples of how motivated, inspired, and prepared for lifelong success students can be after several semesters of college matriculation. Many of these great leaders, entrepreneurs, and trailblazers who never completed college often credit postsecondary education for setting them on a path to success. In fact, the Bill & Melinda Gates Foundation offers the most lucrative scholarship in higher education, the Gates Millennium Scholarship.

The College Completion Glass—Half-Full or Half-Empty? Exploring the Value of Postsecondary Education presents a new paradigm for higher education, one that focuses on the "value added" of postsecondary education as well as on student success beyond the traditional measure of college graduation rates. This chapter provides an overview of how graduation rates are calculated and tracked by the US Department of Education, NCES, and state legislatures, as well as the limitations of these measures.

THE GENESIS OF NATIONAL GRADUATION RATES

On November 9, 1990, the US Congress passed the Student Right-to-Know Act, also known as the Student Right-to-Know and Campus Security Act (P.L. 101-542). Title I, section 103, of the act requires institutions eligible for Title IV funding to disclose completion or graduation rates of certificate- or degree-seeking, full-time students entering an institution to all students and prospective students (McFarland et al., 2017). Furthermore,

> [s]ection 104 requires each institution that participates in any Title IV program and is attended by students receiving athletically related student aid to annually submit a report to the Secretary of Education. This report is to contain, among other things, graduation/completion rates of all students as well as students receiving athletically related student aid by race/ethnicity and gender and by sport, and the average completion or graduation rate for the four most

recent years. These data are also required to be disclosed to parents, coaches, and potential student athletes when the institution offers athletically related student aid. The Graduation Rates component of IPEDS [Integrated Postsecondary Education Data System] was developed specifically to help institutions respond to these requirements. (Ginder, Kelly-Reid, & Mann, 2017, p. B5)

NCES is responsible for collecting, analyzing, and reporting data related to education in the United States and other nations. It fulfills the Student Right-to-Know Act mandate to collect, collate, analyze, and report full and complete statistics on the condition of education in the United States; to conduct and publish reports and specialized analyses of the meaning and significance of such statistics; to assist state and local education agencies in improving their statistical systems; and to review and report on education activities in foreign countries (McFarland et al., 2017).

NCES's IPEDS surveys approximately 7,500 postsecondary institutions, including universities and colleges, as well as institutions offering technical and vocational education beyond the high school level. IPEDS, an annual universe collection that began in 1986, replaced the Higher Education General Information Survey (HEGIS). IPEDS consists of interrelated survey components that provide information on postsecondary institutions, student enrollment, programs offered, degrees and certificates conferred, and both the human and financial resources involved in the provision of institutionally based postsecondary education (McFarland et al., 2017).

THE IPEDS GRADUATION RATE

The IPEDS graduation rate counts completion status as 150 percent of normal program completion time (typically a six-year graduation rate for four-year institutions) at the same institution where the students started their postsecondary education as full-time, first-time, degree- or certificate-seeking undergraduate students in the specified cohort year (Ginder, Kelly-Reid, & Mann, 2017). Transfer students, part-time students, and students who begin college matriculation in terms or semesters other than fall, as well as many mature students, are not counted in the federal IPEDS graduation rates. Students who transfer without completing a degree are counted as noncompleters in the calculation of these rates, regardless of whether they complete a degree at another institution (McFarland et al., 2017).

Also, responding to the IPEDS graduation rate survey (GRS) is wrought with complexities; institutions are required to be aware of which students to include (e.g., Can first-time students attending the previous summer be included?), which students to exclude (e.g., Can students who temporarily stop their studies because of military service be excluded?), and the dates used to compute an accurate graduation rate (National Postsecondary Education

Cooperative, 2010). Additionally, IPEDS collects a 200 percent graduation rate for postsecondary institutions. The 200 percent graduation rate extends the time from 150 percent to 200 percent, which represents an eight-year graduation rate for most four-year institutions. While the 200 percent rate extends the time for degree completion for students at the same institution, it continues to exclude transfer students, part-time students, and students who begin college matriculation in terms or semesters other than fall, as well as many mature students. When the time students were tracked for program completion was extended from within 150 percent of normal time to 200 percent of normal time for the 2007 fall cohort of first-time, full-time freshmen, graduation rates for undergraduates at all four-year institutions only increased from 59.3 percent to 61.6 percent (Ginder, Kelly-Reid, & Mann, 2017).

The IPEDS outcome measure (OM) provides the degree completion and enrollment status of four degree- or certificate-seeking undergraduate student cohorts and eight subcohorts at degree-granting institutions. Student completion rates of reporting institutions are collected at the four-year, six-year, and eight-year status points after the students entered the reporting institution. The enrollment status of students who did not earn an award is also collected after eight years of matriculation.

WHAT IS THE US GRADUATION RATE?

About 59 percent of students who began seeking a bachelor's degree at a four-year institution in fall 2009 completed that degree within six years; the graduation rate was higher for females than for males (62 percent vs. 56 percent; McFarland et al., 2017). Between 2010 and 2015, the overall six-year graduation rate for first-time, full-time students who began seeking a bachelor's degree at four-year degree-granting institutions increased by 1 percent, from 58 percent (for students who began their studies in 2004 and graduated within six years) to 59 percent (for students who began their studies in 2009 and graduated within six years) (see figure 1.1). Six-year graduation rates were higher in 2015 than in 2010 at public institutions (59 percent vs. 56 percent) and private nonprofit institutions (66 percent vs. 65 percent) but lower at private for-profit institutions (23 percent vs. 29 percent). In addition, the six-year graduation rate for females increased during this period (from 61 percent to 62 percent), and the six-year graduation rate for males was approximately 1 percent higher (56 percent in both years; McFarland et al., 2017, p. 270).

The Condition of Education 2017 reports that six-year graduation rates were highest at institutions that were the most selective (i.e., had the lowest acceptance rates) and were lowest at institutions that were the least selective

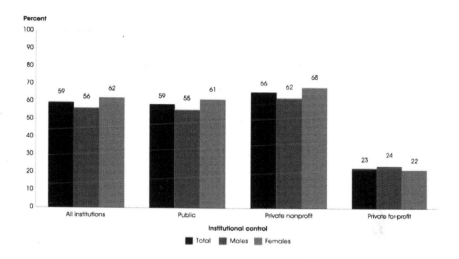

Figure 1.1. Graduation rate within 150 percent of normal time (six years) from first institutions attended for first-time, full-time bachelor's-degree-seeking students at four-year postsecondary institutions, by control of institution and sex. Cohort entry year 2009. *Source:* US Department of Education, National Center for Education Statistics (2016). See table 326.10, "Integrated Postsecondary Education Data System (IPEDS), Winter 2015–16," graduation rates component.

Note: Data are for four-year degree-granting postsecondary institutions participating in Title IV federal financial aid programs. Graduation rates include students receiving bachelor's degrees from their initial institution of attendance only. Although rounded numbers are displayed, the figures are based on unrounded estimates.

(i.e., had open admissions policies). For example, at four-year institutions with open admissions policies, only 32 percent of students completed a bachelor's degree within six years, but at four-year institutions where the acceptance rate was less than 25 percent of applicants, the six-year graduation rate was 88 percent (McFarland et al., 2017). Only about four in ten (42 percent) black students who start college as first-time, full-time freshmen earn bachelor's degrees from those institutions within six years—a rate 22 percentage points below that of their white peers (see figure 1.2).

Chapter 5, "HBCUs, MSIs, and the College Completion Game," further explores gaps and disparities in graduation rates by race and ethnicity. Specifically, what impact, if any, does the IPEDS graduation rate survey methodology have on race and ethnicity gaps in college completion data across institutions and institution types?

While the current IPEDS reporting system works well for some institutions, such as residential colleges that educate almost entirely traditional-age

Six Year Graduation Rates at Four Year Institutions (2014)

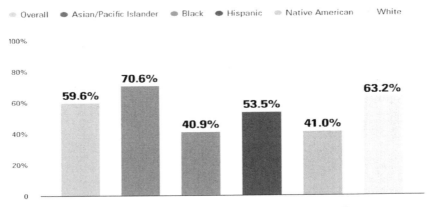

Source: U.S. Department of Education, National Center for Education Statistics, IPEDS, Fall 2008 starting cohort. Table 326.10

Figure 1.2.   Six-year graduation rates at four-year institutions (2014). *Source: US Department of Education, National Center for Education Statistics (2016). See table 326.10, "Integrated Postsecondary Education Data System (IPEDS)," fall 2008 starting cohort.*

college students who enroll full time and stay at one institution, institutions that educate large numbers of students who matriculate at several institutions or who transfer without a degree can easily have a majority of their students not counted by the federal system (Jaschik, 2013).

WHO DOESN'T COUNT?

The American Institutes for Research (AIR) reports that, in 2015, nearly 70,000 students earned an undergraduate credential at a college or university that, according to the US Department of Education, had a 0 percent graduation rate. Another 2.6 million students were new enrollees in fall 2014, but regardless of whether they ever complete the certificate or degree they are hoping to earn, they won't be counted in the graduation rates their college reports to the US Department of Education (Soldner, Smither, Parsons, & Peek, 2016). These 2.6 million students were not first-time, full-time students to be included in the IPEDS cohort but were new students at postsecondary institutions in fall 2014.

AIR estimates that the share of students excluded from IPEDS graduation rate hovers around 50 percent and has increased in 9 of the 10 most recent years of available NCES data. In fact, a 2012 report by the National Student

Clearinghouse Research Center funded by the Lumina Foundation found that nontraditional students, such as those who postpone college enrollment after high school, attend college part time, and/or have full-time jobs, have become the new majority among US college students (Shapiro et al., 2012).

ALTERNATIVES TO IPEDS INCLUDING THE STUDENT ACHIEVEMENT MEASURE (SAM)

According to AIR, several projects have worked to identify better ways to collect, measure, and report information about student persistence and completion, including Transparency by Design; the Voluntary Institutional Metrics Project; the Voluntary System of Accountability; and, most recently, the Student Achievement Measure (SAM; Soldner, Smither, Parsons, & Peek, 2016). The SAM is an improved way to report undergraduate student progress and completion by including a greater proportion of students, as well as tracking students who enroll in multiple higher-education institutions. It tracks student movement across postsecondary institutions to provide a more complete picture of undergraduate student progress and completion within the higher-education system. It is an alternative to the federal graduation rate, which is limited to tracking the completion of first-time, full-time students at one institution. The SAM system is endorsed by the American Association of Community Colleges (AACU), the American Association of State Colleges and Universities (AASCU), the American Council on Education (ACE), the Association of American Universities (AAU), the Association of Public and Land-Grant Universities (APLU), and the National Association of Independent Colleges and Universities (NAICU).

The SAM tracks the progress of students within a cohort over a 6-year (full-time bachelor's-seeking cohorts and associate- or certificate-seeking cohorts) or 10-year (part-time bachelor's-seeking cohorts) time period ending in a summer term. The bachelor's-degree model reports on the percentage of students who

- graduated from the reporting institution;
- are still enrolled at the reporting institution;
- transferred or graduated from one or more subsequent institutions;
- transferred or are still enrolled at a subsequent institution;
- have unknown current enrollment or graduation status (including students who transferred but whose enrollment or graduation status is unknown).

The associate- and certificate-program model reports on the percentage of students who

- graduated from the reporting institution;
- are still enrolled at the reporting institution;
- transferred to one or more subsequent institution (includes students who transferred and are still enrolled, students who transferred and have graduated, and students who transferred but whose enrollment or graduation status is unknown);
- have unknown transfer, current enrollment, or graduation status.

The new IPEDS OM component and the SAM are including more students in persistence and completion rates. The American Institutes for Research points out that, while the IPEDS OM reports on the outcomes of four cohorts that, together, include all of an institution's students (full-time, first-time; full-time, non-first-time; part-time, first-time; and part-time, non-first-time), the SAM provides institutions a similar opportunity, though it makes reporting the outcomes of part-time enrollees optional. Though both approaches demonstrate the possibility to greatly expand the number of students included in persistence and completion metrics, AIR has introduced yet another measurement system for consideration: the inclusive measurement of student outcomes (IMSO) principles (Soldner, Smither, Parsons, & Peek, 2016).

THE NATIONAL STUDENT CLEARINGHOUSE (NSC)

The National Student Clearinghouse database's near-census national coverage of six-year outcomes of enrollments and awarded degrees of first-time, degree-seeking students enhances the traditional graduation rate by reporting in four key ways: (1) student completion anywhere, beyond institutional boundaries, across state lines, and over time; (2) persistence anywhere, not just at the starting institution, for those who have not yet completed but are still pursuing a degree; (3) college outcomes broken out by student age at first entry and enrollment intensity, thus addressing questions about the role of students' varied postsecondary pathways in progress toward national completion goals; and (4) enrollment intensity based on the enrollment status in all terms of enrollment and not just the first term (Shapiro et al., 2012).

According to the National Student Clearinghouse Research Center, by the end of year 4, 39.6 percent had completed a postsecondary credential, while 16.4 percent were no longer enrolled. By the end of year 6, 69.0 percent had graduated, while 20.5 percent had left college without earning a credential (see figure 1.3).

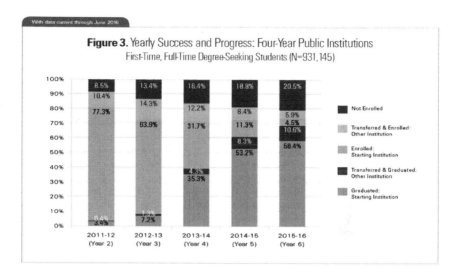

Figure 1.3. Yearly success and progress rates for individuals who began college in fall 2010 as full-time, degree-seeking students at four-year public institutions. *Source:* **National Student Clearinghouse Research Center, 2017.**

THE FUTURE OF THE GRADUATION RATE MEASUREMENT

AIR advocates for the IMSO principles, designed to generate maximum information for students, institutional leaders, and policy makers. If more fully adopted, the three IMSO principles that AIR argues would increase the amount and quality of data about student persistence and completion are:

- **Principle 1:** Include all students. An institution should monitor the persistence and completion outcomes of every student it enrolls, without exception.
- **Principle 2:** Include all persistence and completion outcomes at all institutions. An institution should monitor a student's persistence and completion outcomes even after transfer and know what those specific outcomes are—including continued persistence at a transfer institution or degree completion there. With the continued expansion of the NSC, federated longitudinal data systems, and other data exchanges, it is increasingly possible to monitor the persistence and completion outcomes of virtually every transfer student.
- **Principle 3:** Use a student's perspective of time to report yearly outcomes. An institution should measure students' persistence outcomes in a familiar metric, elapsed calendar time, and collect those outcomes in a way that allows the creation and reporting of metrics annually. It should

be possible to collect (and report on) year 1 outcomes of a cohort of enrollees, for example, within a year of those outcomes having been observed by the institution. (Soldner, Smither, Parsons, & Peek, 2016, pp. 5–6)

In 2016, the Bill & Melinda Gates Foundation partnered with the Institute for Higher Education Policy (IHEP) to develop a metrics framework to represent how leading institutions and states are measuring their performance. The framework includes three core design principles: (1) count all students and institutions; (2) count all outcomes; and (3) costs count. The framework offers a set of metrics that are currently in use by major initiatives to measure institutional performance related to student access, progression, completion, cost, and postcollege outcomes; it highlights metrics in use that examine institutional performance in relation to resources (efficiency) and with respect to diverse populations (equity; Engle, 2016).

To achieve the goal of strengthening data systems, a coalition of organizations in conjunction with the Bill & Melinda Gates Foundation and IHEP is developing a blueprint for improving the national postsecondary data infrastructure with the goals of increasing the data capacity of institutions, continuing to develop robust state data systems, developing a more comprehensive national data system or exchange, and supporting open yet secure access and use of data. The Bill & Melinda Gates Foundation continues to support and fund programs and initiatives to promote college completion and improve data systems to measure and assess student success in postsecondary education.

THE #COUNTALLSTUDENTS CAMPAIGN

In 2016, colleges and universities across the country launched the #Count AllStudents Campaign to share stories of 2016 graduates who transferred or attended college part time and were missing from the federal graduation rate. Through dozens of student vignettes available on the SAM (2013) website and shared on social media, institutions urged the federal government to update its IPEDS graduation rate survey, which only reports outcomes for students who begin college full time and don't transfer.

According to its sponsoring partner, the APLU, the #CountAllStudents campaign has drawn attention to the misleading information portrayed by the federal graduation rate, which is often cited as a sign of institutional performance. Morgan State University (MSU) participated in the #CountAllStudents campaign:

Malcolm Jiles was a student in my Health 100 course at MSU. In 2011, he asked me to write a letter of recommendation for him to transfer to Cornell University. After trying to talk him out of leaving MSU, I did write the letter and send him on his way to another university with his 4.0 cumulative GPA. It was a painful loss, but he kept in touch. He stopped by my office to check in with me in May 2016 and wrote this e-mail to me as a follow-up to our visit. He began at Morgan State University in fall 2010 and finished at Cornell University in spring 2014; his transfer counted against us in our cohort graduation rate at Morgan, and Cornell did not receive credit for his graduation, either. Malcolm wanted me to add his story to the APLU website and campaign #CountAllStudents. His letter stated:

To Whom It May Concern,

I am one of a few African American Cornell University alums only because I transferred from Morgan State University after my first year. I was a proud "Morganite" from August 2010 until May 2011. I graduated from Cornell University in the winter of 2014 with a Bachelor of Science Degree (major was animal science). I am now currently a CUNY laboratory animal technician at the Advanced Science Research Center. I am aware of the fact that MSU graduation rates are low and I was also informed that the government believes that most former students [who took the path I chose] cannot give MSU any credit for my success. Morgan State was my first step into the real world. It was an environment where people had to learn to look out for each other and support their fellow classmates. It was an environment that required me to dedicate myself to my studies so I could achieve a 4.0 GPA. It was an environment that showed me the consequences of settling for less. It was an environment where I was really put to the test to demonstrate my worth to society. It was an environment full of professors who looked forward to not only instructing students, but also to connect[ing] and bond[ing] with students so they can be guided to a path of success. Morgan State gave me the academic values and virtues that I needed to carry on to succeed at an Ivy League like Cornell. Had it not been for caring professors (e.g. Dr. Tiffany Mfume) at Morgan State, I would have never had the opportunity to even chase my dreams of becoming a veterinarian. I never left Morgan State with any kind of saltiness or opposition, for if they had the study I specifically wanted, I would have completed 4 years at this lovely HBCU. Being a student of MSU always makes me proud. I will definitely give MSU a huge amount of gratitude for helping me build the bold, hardened character to succeed anywhere. MSU will always have a special place in my memory and my heart because it is a part of me that I cannot erase, but a part of me that I can thank for shaping me into the successful young black man I am today.

Thank You MSU, Malcolm Xavier Jiles

I hope stories like his will help change the narrative and support the APLU's #CountAllStudents campaign. I can't help but wonder what our graduation rate would be if we counted students who began at Morgan and finished anywhere in the nation, especially if we were to count beyond only six consecutive years of matriculation to include part-time, transfer, and nontraditional students.

THE BOTTOM LINE

Changes are on the horizon for the federal graduation rate. Colleges and universities, professional organizations and associations, foundations and advocacy groups, as well as students themselves, are advocating for change to the existing NCES IPEDS system. Counting and tracking the success of all students—traditional, first-time, full-time freshmen, as well as nontraditional, mature, part-time, and transfer students—across both 2-year and 4-year institutions for 4 years, 6 years, 8 years, and 10 years will add tremendous value and better understanding of postsecondary education. In an environment characterized by rising out-of-pocket college prices and uncertain employment and wage prospects, having accurate information about where that investment is most likely to result in earning a certificate or degree is crucial (Soldner, Smither, Parsons, & Peek, 2016).

REFERENCES

Engle, J. (2016). Answering the call: Institutions and states lead the way toward better measures of postsecondary performance. *Bill & Melinda Gates Foundation*. Retrieved from https://postsecondary.gatesfoundation.org/wp-content/uploads/2016/02/AnsweringtheCall.pdf.

Ginder, S. A., Kelly-Reid, J. E., & Mann, F. B. (2017). *Graduation rates for selected cohorts, 2007–12; student financial aid, academic year 2014–15; and admissions in postsecondary institutions, fall 2015: First look (provisional data)* (NCES 2017-084). Washington, DC: US Department of Education, National Center for Education Statistics. Retrieved from https://nces.ed.gov/pubs2017/2017084.pdf.

Jaschik, S. (2013, June 24). New measure of success. *Inside Higher Ed*. Retrieved from https://www.insidehighered.com/news/2013/06/24/college-associations-introduce-new-ways-measure-student-completion.

McFarland, J., Hussar, B., de Brey, C., Snyder, T., Wang, X., Wilkinson-Flicker, S., Gebrekristos, S., Zhang, J., Rathbun, A., Barmer, A., Bullock Mann, F., & Hinz, S. (2017). *The condition of education 2017* (NCES 2017-144). Washington, DC: US Department of Education, National Center for Education Statistics. Retrieved from https://nces.ed.gov/pubs2017/2017144.pdf.

National Postsecondary Education Cooperative. (2010). *Suggestions for improving the IPEDS graduation rate survey data collection and reporting* (NPEC 2010–832). Prepared by B. Albright for Coffey Consulting, Washington, DC. Retrieved from https://nces.ed.gov/pubs2010/2010832.pdf.

National Student Clearinghouse Research Center. (2017, Spring). *Snapshot report: Yearly success and progress rates (fall 2010 entering cohort)*. Retrieved from https://nscresearchcenter.org/wp-content/uploads/SnapshotReport25.pdf.

Shapiro, D., Dundar, A., Chen, J., Ziskin, M., Park, E., Torres, V., & Chiang, Y. C. (2012). Completing college: A national view of student attainment rates. *National Student Clearing-house*. Retrieved from https://files.eric.ed.gov/fulltext/ED538117.pdf.

Soldner, M., Smither, C., Parsons, K., & Peek, A. (2016, May). Toward improved measure-ment of student persistence and completion. *American Institutes for Research*. Retrieved from https://www.air.org/sites/default/files/downloads/report/Toward-Improved-Measure ment-Persistance-and-Completion-May-2016.pdf.

Student Achievement Measure (SAM). (2013). Retrieved from http://www.student achievementmeasure.org/.

US Department of Education, National Center for Education Statistics. (2016). *Digest of educa-tion statistics: 2016*. Retrieved from https://nces.ed.gov/programs/digest/d16/.

Chapter Two

The College Completion Agenda

During the eight years of the Obama presidency, President Obama repeatedly called for the United States to significantly improve its postsecondary education performance (Bosworth, 2010). In 2010, 42 percent of Americans in the 25-to-34 age range had earned a degree from a two- or four-year institution of higher education (OECD, 2010). In the 1970s, that statistic would have been high enough to make the United States the best-educated country in the world, but America has not kept pace with other countries. In 2010, it was tied for ninth in the world in postsecondary education attainment, according to the Organization of Economic Cooperation and Development's (OECD) *Education at a Glance 2010*. President Obama asked colleges and universities to help the United States retake the lead by increasing that figure to 60 percent by 2020.

AMERICAN RECOVERY AND REINVESTMENT ACT

On February 17, 2009, President Obama signed into law the American Recovery and Reinvestment Act (ARRA) of 2009, historic legislation designed to stimulate the economy, support job creation, and invest in crucial sectors, including education. The ARRA provided $4.35 billion for the Race to the Top Fund, a competitive grant program designed to encourage and reward states that were creating conditions for education innovation and reform and achieving significant improvement in student outcomes, including making substantial gains in student achievement, closing achievement gaps, improving high school graduation rates, and ensuring student preparation for success in college and careers (US Department of Education, 2009).

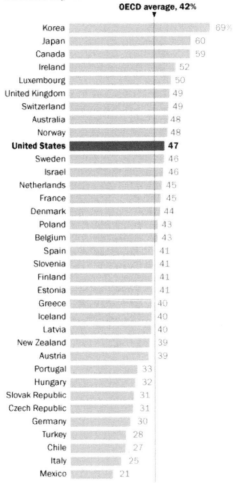

In 2015 the U.S. ranked 10th among OECD countries in college attainment

% of 25- to 34-year-olds completing at least an associate degree

OECD average, 42%

Korea	69%
Japan	60
Canada	59
Ireland	52
Luxembourg	50
United Kingdom	49
Switzerland	49
Australia	48
Norway	48
United States	**47**
Sweden	46
Israel	46
Netherlands	45
France	45
Denmark	44
Poland	43
Belgium	43
Spain	41
Slovenia	41
Finland	41
Estonia	41
Greece	40
Iceland	40
Latvia	40
New Zealand	39
Austria	39
Portugal	33
Hungary	32
Slovak Republic	31
Czech Republic	31
Germany	30
Turkey	28
Chile	27
Italy	25
Mexico	21

Note: Data shown are the share in each country who have completed OECD's definition of short cycle tertiary education.
Source: OECD, Education at a Glance 2016 Table A.1.2

PEW RESEARCH CENTER

Figure 2.1.   As of 2015, the nation ranked 10th among the 35 OECD countries in college attainment.

RACE TO THE TOP

President Obama's Race to the Top Initiative used a competitive grant process to rely on incentives instead of sanctions to drive state reform. According to Patrick McGuinn (2012), three factors contributed to the design and impact of Race to the Top: (1) the enormously difficult task of driving systemic change in a fragmented and decentralized education system, (2) the newness of and political opposition to federal efforts to push systemic education reform on the states, and (3) the weakness of state and federal administrative capacity in education.

Some detractors have labeled the Race to the Top Initiative as a flawed educational reform plan that increases standardization, centralization, and test-based accountability in our nation's schools (Onosko, 2011). Supporters of Race to the Top argue that it has been successful in two areas: (1) creating political cover for state education reformers to innovate, and (2) helping states construct the administrative capacity to implement these innovations effectively (McGuinn, 2012). Arguably, despite its imperfections, Race to the Top generated considerable momentum and impact on the national political discourse around education and resulted in many states enacting major policy changes.

DEPARTMENT OF EDUCATION, COMPLETION, AND COSTS

In March 2011, the US Department of Education released the College Completion Tool Kit, outlining seven low-cost strategies based on promising state and local practices for governors to consider: (1) developing an action plan, (2) embracing performance-based funding, (3) aligning high school standards with college entrance and placement standards, (4) making it easier for students to transfer, (5) using data to drive decision making, (6) accelerating learning and reducing costs, and (7) targeting adult students (Shapiro et al., 2012).

In 2013, President Obama outlined a plan to combat rising college costs and make college affordable for American families by measuring college performance through a new ratings system, with a goal to tie federal student aid to college performance. President Obama's plan aimed to take down barriers that stand in the way of competition and innovation, particularly in the use of new technology, and shine a light on the most cutting-edge college practices for providing high value at low costs (White House, Office of the Press Secretary, 2013).

FIRST IN THE WORLD

The Obama administration's First in the World (FITW) program was designed to support the development, replication, and dissemination of innovative solutions and evidence for what works in addressing persistent and widespread challenges for students who are at risk of not persisting in and completing postsecondary programs, including but not limited to adult learners, working students, part-time students, students from low-income backgrounds, students of color, students with disabilities, and first-generation students. The First in the World grants funded the development and testing of innovative approaches and strategies at colleges and universities to improve college attainment and make higher education more affordable for students and families (US Department of Education, 2014).

The Pew Research Center reports that the nation has made some progress toward the 2020 college completion goal outlined during the Obama years; in March 2009, 41 percent of 25- to 34-year-olds had completed at least an associate degree, compared to March 2016, when 48 percent of young adults had done so (Fry, 2017) (see figure 2.2).

THE LUMINA FOUNDATION

The Lumina Foundation was established in 2000 as an independent, private foundation committed to making opportunities for learning beyond high school available to all. Lumina envisions a system that is easy to navigate, delivers fair results, and meets the nation's need for talent through a broad range of credentials, with a goal of preparing people for informed citizenship and for success in a global economy. Lumina Foundation's "big goal" is to increase the proportion of Americans with high-quality degrees, certificates, and other credentials to 60 percent by 2025. A 2015 Gallup/Lumina poll found that 90 percent of Americans believe it's important to increase the rate of college attainment in America (Lumina Foundation, 2017).

According to Lumina, between now and 2025, about 24.2 million Americans will earn postsecondary credentials, and 16.4 million more need to be added to that total to meet the 2025 "big goal." To produce the 16.4 million additional credentials, Lumina has identified five interconnected priorities for action—big ideas about how to reach Goal 2025 by meeting the needs of the populations whose attainment must increase:

1. a postsecondary learning system where the top priorities are completion of quality credentials, affordability, and closing equity gaps

Progress in increasing college attainment during the Obama years

% of 25- to 34-year-olds completing at least an associate degree

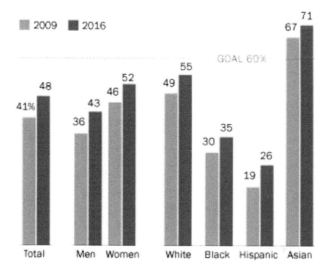

Note: The total and men/women include racial and ethnic groups not separately shown. Whites, blacks and Asians include only non-Hispanics. Hispanics are of any race. Asians include Native Hawaiians and Pacific Islanders.
Source: Pew Research Center analysis of 2009 and 2016 Current Population Survey, Annual Social and Economic Supplements (IPUMS)

PEW RESEARCH CENTER

Figure 2.2. In March 2009, 41 percent of 25- to 34-year-olds had completed at least an associate degree. By March 2016, 48 percent of young adults had done so.

2. a new national system of high-quality postsecondary credentials that makes learning transparent to employers, education providers, and students

3. national expansion of competency-based learning approaches to recognize postsecondary learning however and wherever it is obtained

4. pathways to initial credentials—including certificates and certifications—for adults without postsecondary education
5. an integrated quality-assurance system for postsecondary learning built on data assessing institutional performance regarding financial responsibility, equity, and employability (Lumina Foundation, 2017)

The Lumina Foundation declares that the scale of change needed to be successful in meeting Goal 2025 will require action on the part of numerous policy makers, educators, employers, and individual Americans. Lumina's strategic approach to the work is built on five key organizational capacities: (1) stakeholder engagement, (2) state policy, (3) federal policy, (4) innovation and scale, and (5) impact and metrics. Lumina believes that its impact will be determined by its ability to leverage its organizational resources in all five areas to advance effective solutions on a wide scale for implementation by multiple stakeholders (Lumina Foundation, 2017).

COMPLETE COLLEGE AMERICA (CCA)

Complete College America is a national nonprofit organization that aspires to eliminate achievement gaps in postsecondary education by providing equity of opportunity for all students to complete college degrees and credentials of purpose and value. Through research, advocacy, and technical assistance, CCA helps states put in place its six identified game changers to help all students succeed in college: (1) 15 to Finish, (2) Math Pathways, (3) Co-requisite Support, (4) Momentum Year, (5) Academic Maps with Proactive Advising, and (6) A Better Deal for Returning Adults (Jones, 2015).

Complete College America suggests that, to significantly improve America's postsecondary graduation rate, higher education must be reinvented to meet the needs of the new majority of students, who must balance the jobs they need with the education they desire (Bosworth, 2010). A 2010 CCA study concluded that certificate awards for completion of programs of study of at least one year have significant and consistent labor market value and should count toward national and state postsecondary attainment goals (Bosworth, 2010). Garrison Walters (2012) asserts,

> Colleges and universities need to organize nationally—and in a very visible way—to do three things: (1) embrace the positive aspects of the completion agenda, such as the focus on adult education; (2) promote further efforts at continuous improvement, as in Maryland and Virginia, but include radical outsourcing and collaborative strategies; and (3) develop more systematic research and development projects to improve learning and success to graduation. (p. 38)

STATES AND THE COLLEGE COMPLETION AGENDA

Some describe Complete College America's strategy as a "pressure-punitive" funding model because it is designed to force institutions to change and punish them if they do not (Walters, 2012). According to Walters, former executive director of the South Carolina Commission on Higher Education, states are the principal target of the completion agenda because it is at the state level that political pressure can be most effectively linked to drivers of institutional change. Reyna, Reindl, Witham, and Stanley (2010) observe,

> Recognizing the importance of college completion to the nation's economic vitality, the National Governors Association (NGA) launched an initiative to help all states improve higher education performance. Through Complete to Compete, states work to increase college completion and improve higher education efficiency. To accomplish this objective, states need to collect and report comparable data and implement policies aligned with these goals. (p.7)

The National Governors Association endorses metrics that provide (1) checks to ensure that access to higher education is not sacrificed in favor of completion, (2) a system-wide snapshot of higher-education productivity, and (3) a method to track the growth in the overall level of education in the state.

MARYLAND'S COLLEGE COMPLETION AGENDA

In 2013, Maryland's College Completion Agenda congealed with the passage of Maryland Senate Bill 740, known as the College Readiness and Completion Act. This comprehensive bill included K–12, community college, and four-year components with goals to increase the number of college graduates, increase the rigor and preparation for those people entering a workforce that is demanding greater skills and knowledge, reduce remediation required for students entering community colleges, reduce the cost of college, and close the gap between graduation requirements and college and career readiness.

The four-year components of SB 740 required that pathways and degree plans are in place by the accumulation of 45 credits; limited the number of credits needed to achieve a bachelor of arts or bachelor or science degree to 120 except for unique programs with specific accreditation mandates; required the Maryland Higher Education Commission (MHEC) to develop and implement a statewide transfer agreement whereby at least 60 credits of general education, elective, and major courses transfer; and required postsecondary institutions to dedicate institutional-based financial aid for students who transfer with associate's degrees.

STATE MANDATE OR CHANGE CATALYST?

In 2010, I authored the report Barriers to and Strategies for Student Success, Retention, and Graduation at Morgan State University. *Serving in the role of director of student retention, I identified seven barriers: (1) money (paying for college), (2) requirements for a degree, (3) university policies and procedures, (4) customer service, (5) technology, (6) academic advising, and (7) campus culture. Our new president afforded me the opportunity to present these barriers to him and his leadership team, and he provided overall support and feedback toward eliminating them. However, several of the barriers required coordination across divisions and campus-wide buy-in.*

While the university was on track to address each barrier one by one over time, there was not necessarily a sense of urgency in the larger context of a new president's ambitious global agenda. Then, in 2013, amid all the buzz surrounding Maryland Senate Bill 740, our president appointed the Obstacles to Degree Completion Task Force. Once again, a list of recommendations was submitted to our president to include reducing bachelor's degree programs to 120 credit hours, revising the general education curriculum to include more course options, developing a multidisciplinary degree program to offer flexibility to stopped-out near-completers, implementing professional advising for all first-year students, and providing more flexibility in the transferred courses that count toward general education credits.

With the backing of the mandates presented by Maryland's SB 740, our addenda had the much-needed urgency to make sweeping changes. Without the momentum created by SB 740, the college completion agenda at Morgan State University would not have moved forward as quickly or as effectively. Adoption of the SB 740 mandates and our in-house Obstacles to Degree Completion Task Force recommendations have helped to promote 10-point increases in MSU's retention and graduation rates, from a 63 percent (2006 cohort) to a 73 percent (2015 cohort) retention rate in 2016 and from a 28 percent (2005 cohort) to a 38 percent (2011 cohort) graduation rate in 2017. A push from an external entity or a state mandate can act as a catalyst for institutional change.

FLAWS OF THE COMPLETION AGENDA

Some critics view the completion agenda as an unfunded mandate to do more with less, as an agenda that fails to address the educational, social, and economic challenges without mechanisms for enhancing quality, reducing nonmeritocratic social stratification, or building a new economy:

> The policy disagreement, both nationally and in the states, centers on how policy makers who are overwhelmingly white, college educated, and economi-

cally privileged view and construct the educational prospects of other peoples' children who increasingly are not white, college educated, or economically privileged. One troubling sign of the perceptions is the shift in the goal of realizing greater postsecondary educational achievement. As a result of an ongoing policy push to recognize non-degree educational attainment as success, our focus has, in a very short time, shifted away from college degrees alone to include credentials as well. (Rhoades, 2012, p. 21)

Is there a tension between college access and college completion? One shortcut to improving completion rates is for a college to become more selective in the students it admits. Pell Grant recipients in bachelor's-degree programs who have an A-average high school GPA are almost twice as likely to graduate within six years as students with a B-average high school GPA (72.3 percent vs. 37.9 percent); Pell Grant recipients with the highest admissions test scores are more than twice as likely to graduate in six years as students with the lowest admissions test scores (Kantrowitz, 2012). Redirecting Pell Grant program funding toward colleges with greater graduation rates, as the Obama administration proposed, could lead to a decline in college access by financially incentivizing colleges to become more selective and admit fewer high-risk students.

Kantrowitz (2012) reminds policy makers that "higher-risk students, by definition, are less likely to graduate and will require more financial aid to finish than lower risk students. Increasing graduation rates by excluding higher-risk students from the denominator does not increase the number of graduating students in the numerator." In 2009, the bachelor's-degree attainment by age 24 for dependent students from the bottom half of the income distribution was 12.0 percent; however, their counterparts from the top half of the income distribution attained bachelor's degrees at a 58.8 percent rate (Nichols, 2011). This differential represents a 46.8 percent gap in bachelor's-degree attainment based on family income.

MEETING THE GOAL

Andrew Howard Nichols (2011), author of *Pell Institute for the Study of Opportunity in Higher Education*, argues that reaching the 2020 goal would require aggressive implementation of a set of reforms and policies largely focused on assisting the students, schools, teachers, and communities that need the most assistance and should involve but not be limited to

1. setting and tracking goals to reduce income-based disparities on key educational outcomes related to the 2020 goal;
2. funneling federal dollars, such as Title I funds, to the low-income, underperforming students who need it most;

3. protecting the Pell Grant against cuts that will reduce college access for low-income students;

4. increasing supplemental college access and support services for low-income students throughout the educational pipeline. (p. 6)

According to Nichols, these recommendations would help the nation reduce income-based inequalities in educational attainment and make progress toward the 2020 completion goal.

Evenbeck and Johnson (2012) advise that the completion agenda needn't be pitted against the promising reforms that have been made in postsecondary education. They recommend that colleges and universities articulate and support high expectations, involve students in their learning, and provide assessment and feedback while engaging in evidence-based decision making to identify which innovations are most effective for cultivating competencies in students that will ensure their success as citizens and in the workplace.

THE BOTTOM LINE

In essence, the nation's college completion agenda proposes to return the United States to global prominence in degree attainment. Whether it's the 60 by 2020 goal set by the Obama administration, the Lumina Foundation's 60 by 2025 goal, or a goal established by a state legislature, postsecondary institutions are under pressure to increase graduation rates and produce well-prepared, high-quality graduates. Success in meeting these completion goals, however, will require public funding, institutional reforms, and updated policies; otherwise, the college completion agenda could fizzle and be perceived as nothing more than an insurmountable mandate.

REFERENCES

Bosworth, B. (2010, December). Certificates count: An analysis of sub-baccalaureate certificates. *Complete College America*. Retrieved from https://files.eric.ed.gov/fulltext/ED536837.pdf.

College Readiness and Completion Act of 2013. (2013). *Maryland Senate bill 740*. Retrieved from http://mgaleg.maryland.gov/2013RS/bills/sb/sb0740f.pdf.

Evenbeck, S., & Johnson, K. E. (2012). Students must not become victims of the completion agenda. *Liberal Education, 98*(1), 26–33.

Fry, R. (2017). U.S. still has a ways to go in meeting Obama's goal of producing more college grads. *Pew Research Center*. Retrieved from http://www.pewresearch.org/fact-tank/2017/01/18/u-s-still-has-a-ways-to-go-in-meeting-obamas-goal-of-producing-more-college-grads.

Jones, S. (2015). The game changers: Strategies to boost college completion and close attainment gaps. *Change: The Magazine of Higher Learning, 47*(2), 24–29.

Kantrowitz, M. (2012). The college completion agenda may sacrifice college access for low-income, minority and other at-risk students. *FinAid*. Retrieved from http://www.finaid.org/educators/20120910completionagenda.pdf.

Lumina Foundation. (2017). Lumina Foundation strategic plan for 2017 to 2020. Retrieved from https://www.luminafoundation.org/files/resources/strategic-plan-2017-to-2020-apr17.pdf.

McGuinn, P. (2012). Stimulating reform: Race to the Top, competitive grants and the Obama education agenda. *Educational Policy, 26*(1), 136–59.

Nichols, A. H. (2011, May). Developing 20/20 vision on the 2020 degree attainment goal: The threat of income-based inequality in education. *Pell Institute for the Study of Opportunity in Higher Education.* Retrieved from https://files.eric.ed.gov/fulltext/ED523776.pdf.

Onosko, J. (2011). Race to the Top leaves children and future citizens behind: The devastating effects of centralization, standardization, and high stakes accountability. *Democracy and Education, 19*(2), 1.

Organization for Economic Cooperation and Development (OECD). (2010). *Highlights from education at a glance 2010.* Retrieved from http://www.aic.lv/bolona/2010/Sem09-10/Socdim_Nicosia/highlights_ed_glance_2010.pdf.

Reyna, R., Reindl, T., Witham, K., & Stanley, J. (2010, October). Complete to compete: Common college completion metrics technical guide. *NGA Center for Best Practices.* Retrieved from https://files.eric.ed.gov/fulltext/ED516183.pdf.

Rhoades, G. (2012). The incomplete completion agenda: Implications for academe and the academy. *Liberal Education, 98*(1), 18–25.

Shapiro, D., Dundar, A., Chen, J., Ziskin, M., Park, E., Torres, V., & Chiang, Y. C. (2012). Completing college: A national view of student attainment rates. *National Student Clearinghouse.* Retrieved from https://files.eric.ed.gov/fulltext/ED538117.pdf.

US Department of Education. (2009, November). Race to the Top program: Executive summary. *Race to the Top Fund.* Retrieved from https://www2.ed.gov/programs/racetothetop/executive-summary.pdf.

US Department of Education. (2014, May 15). U.S. Department of Education announces $75 million First in the World competition [Press release]. Retrieved from https://www.ed.gov/news/press-releases/us-department-education-announces-75-million-first-world-competition.

Walters, G. (2012). It's not so easy: The completion agenda and the states. *Liberal Education, 98*(1), 34–39.

White House, Office of the Press Secretary. (2013, August 22). Fact sheet on the president's plan to make college more affordable: A better bargain for the middle class (Press release). Retrieved from https://obamawhitehouse.archives.gov/the-press-office/2013/08/22/fact-sheet-president-s-plan-make-college-more-affordable-better-bargain-.

Chapter Three

The Politics of College Rankings

College rankings such as those published annually by *U.S. News & World Report*, also known as *Best Colleges*, can positively affect an institution's admissions outcomes, resource attainment, and future reputation; however, the positive association between rankings and resource attainment has increased concerns among the higher-education community regarding the "dysfunctions" of rankings (Kim, 2018). According to Kim, rankings encourage some colleges and universities to spend more, moving resources from educational activities to research, amenities and facilities, and administrative expenditures.

Globally, college rankings have become a manifestation of what is known as the worldwide "battle for excellence"; rankings have been used to determine the status of individual institutions, assess the quality and performance of the higher-education system, and gauge global competitiveness (Hazelkorn, 2015). American trends show a steady rise in tuition and fees across all sectors of higher education, persistent state disinvestment, and concern over educational quality and workforce preparation by the public and employers alike (Espinosa, Crandall, & Tukibayeva, 2014). These trends undergird the need for postsecondary education to focus on affordability, quality, and accountability. The question is, Do the current college rankings adequately address the issues of affordability, quality, and accountability?

THE HISTORY OF COLLEGE RANKINGS

The origins of the current college rankings date back to 1900, when "Where We Get Our Best Men" was first published to focus on the number of distinguished men who attended, graduated from, or were faculty at specific institutions (Maclean, 1900). In 1910, the American Association of Universities requested the Bureau of Education to publish a ranking system to rate the quality of US colleges. Both President William Taft and President Woodrow Wilson declined to release the outcomes-based study and make the rankings public (Webster, 1986). In 1924, the first rankings focusing on peer review and institutional reputation were released by the North Central Association of Schools and Colleges. In 1966, the *Cartter Report: An Assessment of Quality in Graduate Education* was released using the most comprehensive methodology to date; it was praised by the national press, and consequently reputational rankings became the norm in postsecondary education (Magoun, 1966).

The first undergraduate ranking study using reputational methodology was the *Chicago Sunday Tribune* article by Chesly Manly in 1957. Manly's rankings rated the whole institution on undergraduate quality and listed the top 10 universities, coeducational colleges, men's colleges, and women's colleges (Alstyne, 1982). In 1983, *U.S. News & World Report* published the first version of *Best Colleges*, ranking undergraduate institutions according to Carnegie classification. *U.S. News* first surveyed college presidents, asking them to name top undergraduate institutions, but then in 1998, *U.S. News* expanded its raters to include academic deans and admissions officers (Sanoff, 2007). *Money* published its first annual *America's Best College Buys* issue in 1990, ranking colleges based on value and quality per dollar of tuition (Stuart, 1995). In 2008, *Forbes*, in partnership with the Center for College Affordability and Productivity, began publishing its rankings based on academic outcomes and the quality of education and achievement.

In 2005, Times Higher Education (THE) published its first *World University Rankings Top 300*, listing the best global universities based on teaching, research, knowledge transfer, and international outlook (Jöns & Hoyler, 2013). Jöns and Hoyler argue that the emergence of global rankings reflects a scalar shift in the geopolitics and geoeconomics of higher education, from the national to the global, that prioritizes academic practices and discourses conducted in particular places and fields of research. Their analysis illustrates how the substantial variation in ranking criteria produces not only necessarily partial but also very specific global geographies of higher education. Myers and Robe (2009) recognize that, "while the purpose and design of academic quality rankings has evolved during the century since their creation, their history teaches one clear lesson: college rankings fill a strong consumer demand for information about institutional quality, and as such, are here to stay for the foreseeable future" (p. 5).

U.S. NEWS & WORLD REPORT RANKINGS

Since its inaugural issue in 1983, the annual *U.S. News & World Report* "America's Best Colleges" issue has become the nation's de facto higher-education accountability system, evaluating colleges and universities on a common scale and creating strong incentives for institutions to do things that raise their ratings (Carey, 2006). Unfortunately, the *U.S. News & World Report* rankings system often promotes colleges and universities that are well known, wealthy, and more selective in their admissions processes. The rankings fail to assess how well colleges and universities educate their students or prepare them for success after college in graduate school, in careers, or in communities.

There often are many questions and concerns about how *U.S. News*'s *Best Colleges* rankings are calculated. In 2015, Morse, Brooks, and Mason provided a detailed explanation in the publication "How *U.S. News* Calculated the 2016 Best Colleges Rankings":

> Regionally accredited schools are categorized by their mission, which is derived from the breakdown of types of higher education institutions as refined by the Carnegie Foundation for the Advancement of Teaching in 2010. The Carnegie classification, which is used extensively by higher education researchers, has been the basis of the *Best Colleges* ranking category system since the first rankings were published in 1983. . . . Once schools have been divided by category, we gather data from each college on up to 16 indicators of academic excellence. Each factor is assigned a weight that reflects our judgment about how much that measure matters. Finally, the colleges and universities in each category are ranked against their peers, based on their composite weighted score. Most of the data come from the colleges. In 2015, 92.7 percent of the *U.S. News* 1,376 ranked colleges and universities we surveyed returned their statistical information during our spring and summer 2015 data collection window. For colleges that were eligible to be ranked but refused to fill out the *U.S. News* statistical survey in the spring and summer of 2015, we have made extensive use of the statistical data those institutions were required to report to the National Center for Education Statistics, including such factors as SAT and ACT scores, acceptance rates, number of faculty, student–faculty ratios and graduation and retention rates. These schools are footnoted as non-responders. The indicators we use to capture academic quality fall into a number of categories: assessment by administrators at peer institutions, retention of students, faculty resources, student selectivity, financial resources, alumni giving, graduation rate performance and, for National Universities and National Liberal Arts Colleges only, high school counselor ratings of colleges. (p. 3)

THE *U.S. NEWS* RANKING FORMULA

U.S. News asserts that its indicators include input measures that reflect a college's student body, its faculty, and its financial resources, along with outcome measures that signal how well the institution does its job of educating students. *U.S. News* weights their ranking formula as follows: undergraduate academic reputation (22.5 percent), retention (22.5 percent), faculty resources (20 percent), student selectivity (12.5 percent), financial resources (10 percent), graduation rate (7.5 percent), and alumni giving rate (5 percent).

Morse, Brooks, and Mason (2015) explain *U.S. News*'s undergraduate academic reputation criterion:

> The *U.S. News* ranking formula gives significant weight to the opinions of those in a position to judge a school's undergraduate academic excellence. The academic peer assessment survey allows top academics—presidents, provosts and deans of admissions—to account for intangibles at peer institutions, such as faculty dedication to teaching. In 2015, in order to get another set of important opinions on National Universities and National Liberal Arts Colleges, *U.S. News* also surveyed 2,200 counselors at public high schools, each of which was a gold, silver or bronze medal winner in a recent edition of the *U.S. News Best High Schools* rankings, as well as 400 college counselors at the largest independent schools. The counselors represent nearly every state and the District of Columbia. (p. 4)

The retention measure has two components:

1. Six-year graduation rate (80 percent)
2. First-year retention rate (20 percent)

The faculty resources criterion used six factors from the 2014–2015 academic year to assess a school's commitment to instruction:

1. The proportion of classes with fewer than 20 students (30 percent)
2. The proportion with 50 or more students (10 percent)
3. The average faculty salary, plus benefits, during the 2013–2014 and 2014–2015 academic years, adjusted for regional differences in the cost of living using indexes from the consulting firm Runzheimer International (35 percent)
4. The proportion of professors with the highest degree in their fields (15 percent)
5. The student–faculty ratio (5 percent)
6. The proportion of faculty who are full time (5 percent)

The student selectivity measure has three components:

1. The admissions test scores for all enrollees who took the critical reading and math portions of the SAT and the composite ACT score (65 percent)
2. The proportion of enrolled first-year students at national universities and national liberal arts colleges who graduated in the top 10 percent of their high school classes or the proportion of enrolled first-year students at regional universities and regional colleges who graduated in the top quarter of their classes (25 percent)
3. The acceptance rate, or the ratio of students admitted to applicants (10 percent)

U.S. News measures financial resources by using the average spending per student on instruction, research, services, and related educational expenditures; spending on sports, dorms, and hospitals doesn't count (Morse, Brooks, & Mason, 2015). *U.S. News* measures the difference between a school's six-year graduation rate for the class that entered in a cohort year and the rate predicted for the class. If the school's actual graduation rate for the entering class is higher than the rate *U.S. News* predicted for that same class, then the college is enhancing achievement, or overperforming. If a school's actual graduation rate is lower than the *U.S. News* prediction, then it is underperforming. The alumni giving rate reflects the average percentage of living alumni with bachelor's degrees who gave to their school, which is an indirect measure of student satisfaction.

In sum, a college's *Best Colleges* rank is calculated by the weighted sum of its standardized scores and then rescaled so that the top college in each category receives a value of 100; the other colleges' weighted scores are calculated as a proportion of that top score. Final scores are rounded to the nearest whole number and ranked in descending order. Colleges that are tied appear in alphabetical order and are marked as tied on all ranking tables. Detailed methodology for each of the categories of *U.S. News Best Colleges* is outlined on its website at www.usnews.com/education/best-colleges/articles/rankings-methodologies.

U.S. NEWS BEST COLLEGES BACKLASH

One consistent criticism of *Best Colleges* is how its rankings incentivize postsecondary institutions to spend more time and more money on branding and reputation, whether it's in the best interest of institutions to invest valuable and often limited resources to raise rankings or not. Results of a 2014 study show that, for a university ranked in the mid-30s in the *U.S. News &*

World Report, it would take a significant amount of additional resources, directed in a very focused way, to become a top-ranked national university and that rank changes of up to four points should be considered "noise" (Gnolek, Falciano, & Kuncl, 2014). In fact, a 2015 article, "Moving Up in the *U.S. News & World Report* Rankings," reports that, for a college or university ranked in the mid-30s, it would cost \$112 million annually to move into the top 20 in the rankings (Martin, 2015). Colleges should not focus their efforts on improving their rankings but instead should focus on meeting other strategic goals.

In 1995, Reed College refused to participate in the *U.S. News* annual survey. Reed College openly questioned the methodology and usefulness of college rankings, even as they were ranked in the top 10 list of liberal arts colleges (Diver, 2005). According to Diver, from 1995 to 2005, while boycotting *U.S. News*'s *Best Colleges*, the number of applicants to Reed College increased by 27 percent, and the quality of entering students, as indicated by both conventional SAT and GPA measures and Reed's internal "reader rating" system, steadily increased to far higher than suggested by its former nominal ranking in the *U.S. News* pecking order. In 1996, students of Stanford University founded FUNC (Forget *U.S. News* Coalition) in support of Reed College's decision not to participate in *U.S. News*'s *Best Colleges*. Students argued that ranking the value of college education with a single number was an oversimplification of a complex assessment (Smith, 2012).

In 1997, the president of Alma College, Alan Stone, asked 480 colleges to boycott the *U.S. News* survey in response to *U.S. News* revealing that 84 percent of respondents from 158 colleges were admittedly unfamiliar with some of the institutions they were asked to rate (Machung, 1998). Only 5 percent of the 480 colleges contacted agreed to participate in Alma's boycott.

During a 2007 annual meeting of liberal arts college presidents, nearly 80 presidents pledged to not participate in the *U.S. News* reputational survey section, which comprises 25 percent of an institution's rating. The editor of *U.S. News* issued a response stating that reputational surveys were important for measuring intangibles that can't be measured through statistical data (Finder, 2007).

RATINGS VS. RANKINGS:
THE OBAMA SCORECARD

The Obama administration's College Scorecard is a database that focuses on a college's graduation rate, graduates' median earnings 10 years after graduation, and the percentage of students paying back their college loans (Stewart, 2015). The College Scorecard website lists commonly available information, like each college's location and enrollment size; however, the Scorecard adds information that was previously difficult or impossible to find, such as average net tuition for financial-aid recipients, student-loan-repayment rates, and the earnings of graduates (Huntington-Klein, 2016). The College Scorecard obtains data from the tax returns of students who receive federal financial aid, including grants and loans. Because most students from high-income families do not receive federal aid, they are excluded from the Scorecard data.

Although the College Scorecard is publicly available, the Scorecard is less well established and less well known than *U.S. News*'s *Best Colleges*. A Google Trends comparison of the search terms "*U.S. News* College Rankings" and "College Scorecard" shows that the *U.S. News* search term beats the Scorecard by about two to one since the launch of the Scorecard in 2015 (Huntington-Klein, 2016). Huntington-Klein's 2016 study found that, even though the Scorecard led people to search more often for high-earnings, high-graduation-rate, and low-tuition colleges as intended, the effect was extremely small. The Scorecard had only small effects on search patterns or aggregate search activity and would need to recruit many more users in order to make a meaningful impact on aggregate (Google) search behavior and drive more interest toward high-performing colleges.

While the Obama administration's College Scorecard adds potentially valuable information to the data and assessments that are already available, it suffers from many of the same flaws that afflict nearly every other college-ranking system (Stewart, 2015). Critics of the College Scorecard have outlined the following concerns: (1) data inaccuracies and misuse, (2) incorrect focus on a simplistic form of college and university value, (3) institutional behavior in the years following its rollout, (4) the notion that the same tool can be used both to drive accountability and to offer consumer information when the information needed by policy makers and students is very different, and (5) the idea that the scorecard will become yet another college and university ranking (Espinosa, Crandall, & Tukibayeva, 2014).

Whitehurst and Chingos (2015) also identify five limitations of the College Scorecard: (1) The salary data are based only on students receiving federal student aid, and thus they potentially produce biased earnings averages by excluding significant numbers of students. (2) The salary data are credited to any institution a student attended with federal student aid, regardless of whether it was for a full-degree program or only a single semester. (3) The salary data are not provided at the level of program of preparation, which is likely a much more important driver of salaries than the overall institution. (4) The salary data are strongly correlated with students' background upon admission, which is not taken into account in the Scorecard. (5) The lack of plans for stewardship of the Scorecard effort presents the risk that it will be a one-time effort. Collins, Jenkins, Strzelecka, Gasman, Wang, and Nguyen (2014) note,

Capturing the complex factors that influence student performance in only a few metrics is challenging; however, continuing the dialogue about refining and improving these metrics to effectively reflect the performance will lead to a more effective system of incentives. Future versions of the College Scorecard would most benefit students and institutions if measurable indicators speak to the priorities of underrepresented students, incorporate customization based on characteristics unique to students, and use this information to develop a performance funding model that supports institutions that enroll and graduate non-traditional students. (p. 11)

PAYSCALE RANKINGS

In 2007, the compensation data firm PayScale began publishing data on the colleges whose graduates earned the highest salaries. Its annually published *College Salary Report* provides prospective college students with information in reference to postgraduation earning power.

In 2017, PayScale surveyed more than 2.3 million graduates of more than 2,700 colleges and universities for the 2017–2018 *College Salary Report*; respondents were asked to report their pay, major, highest degree earned, and associate or bachelor's school name where appropriate. PayScale uses the data from the annual survey to rank colleges, universities, and courses of study by future earning potential; it calculates and ranks the average return on investment for a college and the percentage of graduates holding jobs with "high meaning." Detailed methodology for the PayScale *College Salary Report* is outlined on its website at www.payscale.com/college-salary-report/methodology.

Rankings based on salaries, like PayScale's ratings, could advantage institutions specializing in majors that lead to high-paying jobs in such fields as engineering, computer science, and mathematics and, by the same token, disadvantage institutions that focus on socially oriented careers that are not as lucrative, such as teaching, social work, and nursing (Klein, 2015). According to Stewart (2013), there's a fairly high correlation between the reputation- and selectivity-weighted rankings of *U.S. News* and the future earnings measures of PayScale, with Ivy League graduates doing quite well by both measures. However, many liberal arts colleges suffer in the comparison between *U.S. News*'s *Best Colleges* and the PayScale *College Salary Report* rankings, including some prestigious institutions like Oberlin and Colorado College, who both rank high in *Best Colleges* but much lower on PayScale.

Most experts agree that the PayScale report has improved since its inception; still, some of the PayScale metric's fundamental flaws remain: Because the company bases its data on voluntary survey reports, its samples for certain colleges and majors may not be representative (Lederman, 2017). PayScale's institutional rankings continue to be heavily influenced by the composition of an institution's programs, favoring institutions whose programs lean toward high-paying fields.

In 2012, the analytics manager for PayScale, Katie Bardaro, responded to critics directly in a blog post about the PayScale college ROI rankings. Bardaro states that the PayScale methodology is far more complicated than a simple difference between the cost of attending and the earnings of alumni. She offers the following retorts to critics: (1) PayScale serves as an impartial source of information and would never inflate ratings in order to publicize its rankings. (2) PayScale provides two versions of the rankings (with and without average financial amounts) so that individuals can choose the version that applies to their specific circumstances. (3) The exclusion of graduate students in the PayScale ranking is intentional due to the difficulty in discerning earnings that reflect undergraduate education versus those that are a result of graduate education. (4) PayScale calculates median pay for a school's alumni by using profiles in its database for bachelor's-degree graduates from that school provided directly by alumni, not by using industry averages nor alumni data provided by the schools. Bardaro maintains that the majority of criticism PayScale receives comes from institutions that perform poorly in the ROI rankings.

BROOKINGS RANKINGS

In 2015, the Brookings Institution, a think tank in Washington, DC, published college rankings to measure the "value added" of colleges and universities. Drawing on government and private sources, the Brookings rankings compare what graduates would be expected to earn given their entering characteristics with what they actually earn after graduating (see figure 3.1). Brookings' value-added calculation captures the benefits that accrue from aspects of college quality that can be measured, such as graduation rates and the market value of the skills a college teaches, as well as other harder-to-measure aspects (Kulkarni & Rothwell, 2015).

JUST CHOOSE A COLLEGE FROM THE ONLINE RANKINGS

Just about a decade ago, I had a student share a story with me of how she "ended up" at Morgan State University. It was a sad story because she had been led to believe that Morgan was not a viable and competitive option for her undergraduate studies. This young lady had struggled in high school and admittedly had not made the best choices when it came to time management and study outside of the classroom. She also had been distracted from her high school studies by a couple of stressful, personal family matters.

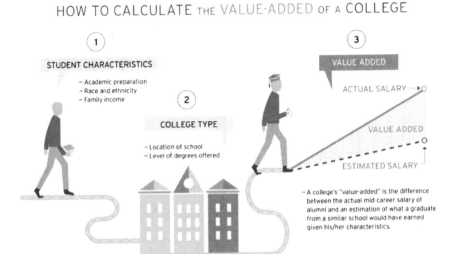

HOW TO CALCULATE THE VALUE-ADDED OF A COLLEGE

(1)

STUDENT CHARACTERISTICS
- Academic preparation
- Race and ethnicity
- Family income

(2)

COLLEGE TYPE
- Location of school
- Level of degrees offered

(3)

VALUE ADDED

ACTUAL SALARY

VALUE ADDED

ESTIMATED SALARY

– A college's "value-added" is the difference between the actual mid-career salary of alumni and an estimation of what a graduate from a similar school would have earned given his/her characteristics.

Figure 3.1. Brookings' value-added calculation. *Source:* **Kulkarni & Rothwell (2015).**

During her required junior-year visit with her high school guidance counselor, she asked about recommendations for colleges, and her guidance counselor recommended that she just check the rankings websites for the best colleges in the state of Maryland or in a particular region, if she wanted to move away from home. She excitedly did her research and found that both Cornell University and Bucknell University offered the types of academic programs she was most interested in. They both had great rankings, with solid reputations to meet her high expectations.

What the guidance counselor failed to discuss with her was her own lack of admissibility to these institutions. This young lady wasted time and money in application fees to apply to Cornell and Bucknell Universities, only to get rejected by both institutions. This young lady did not have high SAT scores, nor had she earned a grade point average of 3.0 or above in high school. By simply referring her to online college rankings without providing the context of her own college preparation and admissibility, her self-confidence and expectations were undermined by her guidance counselor's recommendation.

Like many historically black colleges and universities (HBCUs), Morgan State University has alternative admissions programs, including a six-week summer bridge program for students who are less prepared to have intense, intrusive support in the transition and onboarding process. She was able to be admitted on a conditional basis through MSU's six-week summer bridge program. The question she asked me was why her guidance counselor in Baltimore did not recommend Morgan State University to her from the beginning. If not for a friend of her family recommending that she not give up and contact me at Morgan State University, she could have settled into the notion that college was not an option for her based on her rejections from highly ranked institutions.

WHAT'S WRONG WITH COLLEGE RANKINGS?

In general, irrespective of the specific ranking model or formula, there are innate flaws implicit in all postsecondary education rankings. Because college rankings use quantification as the basis for determining quality and performance, they often grant privilege to older, well-resourced universities, which are highly selective in their recruitment of students and faculty and whose comparative advantages have accumulated over time (Hazelkorn, 2015).

In fact, rankings, themselves, can drive up college costs because the formulas used in calculating rankings reward colleges that spend more money, inevitably resulting in colleges raising their tuition to cover growing costs (Tierney, 2013). Additionally, there are a number of consequences to rankings-influenced decision making, some of which can be positive but most of which have negative implications for low-income student access to the nation's top colleges and universities (Espinosa, Crandall, & Tukibayeva, 2014). Stewart (2015) summarizes,

> The bottom line is that no ranking system or formula can really answer the question of what college a student should attend. Getting into a highly selective, top-ranked college may confer bragging rights, status and connections, but it doesn't necessarily contribute to a good education or lifelong success, financial or otherwise. (p. 5)

There, too, are specific flaws inherent in the *U.S. News* ranking model. For example, results from a 2016 study suggest that the *U.S. News* prediction method for graduation rates underestimates the difficulties of students in STEM disciplines to graduate at the same rate as students with comparable characteristics in non-STEM disciplines. The results show that the graduation rates of the most STEM-focused institutions underperform the predicted rates of all other institutions, with a five-year net difference of 5 percent (Wills, 2016).

Additionally, when institutions are found to have submitted faulty data and are removed from their ranking by *U.S. News*, the response by *U.S. News* is to assert that it is the responsibility of the colleges and universities ranked to ensure the accuracy of their information; universities are sent the data to review after they have been submitted (Jaschik, 2018). While colleges and universities love to highlight their rankings success, they are less likely to share the news that their rankings have been removed due to the submission of incorrect information to *U.S. News* or other ranking organizations.

One perception of college rankings is that they have a direct effect on the college-admissions process. However, a 2016 study found no evidence that college rankings are correlated with the number of admissions applications received by a Historically Black College or University (HBCU), the acceptance rate of an HBCU, the admissions yield of an HBCU, or the SAT scores of incoming students at an HBCU (Jones, 2016). While college rankings do not necessarily affect admissions data for some institution types, for other institution types, rankings can have a direct effect on admissions, retention, and graduation data. Many Ivy League schools have graduation rates as high as 98 percent, with students choosing to remain at these elite institutions, even though the student experience may be better at less-expensive public institutions with much lower graduation rates; this dynamic is a result of the power of branding (Lockwood & Hadd, 2007). Hazelkorn (2015) asserts,

> By highlighting reputational advantage, rankings have affected all higher education institutions—even those which had previously been sheltered by history, mission or governance. Higher education institutions are transformed into strategic knowledge intensive corporations, engaged in positional competition, balanced fragilely between their current and their preferred rank. High-ranked and not-ranked, international-facing and regionally-focused, all institutions have been drawn into the global knowledge market. By granting visibility to some institutions, rankings have become an important tool for strategic positioning and global branding. (p. 29)

VALUE ADDED BY RANKINGS?

Arguably, there are some benefits to college-ranking systems, including promoting excellence in higher education, encouraging competition between colleges that can result in better performance, discouraging stagnation of postsecondary institutions, and meeting the public demand for comparable information about the colleges that students and families invest thousands of dollars in annually (Myers & Robe, 2009). Goglio (2016) concludes that, given the coexistence of different needs, expectations, and priorities that characterize each of the stakeholders involved in college rankings, the search for the best single ranking with the "one size fits all" approach is not the most appropriate when dealing with university rankings. Rather, the field may better benefit from a plurality of university rankings, each one serving different yet equally important functions and answering different demand niches. Myers and Robe (2009) conclude, "Higher education cannot make college rankings go away, but increased transparency and cooperation could lead to rankings that better promote true academic quality than any that have come before" (p. 43).

THE BOTTOM LINE

The most popular college rankings largely are the result of positive branding, student selectivity, college spending and endowments, and graduation rates. Therefore, in order to advance in college rankings, postsecondary institutions must invest in marketing and improving the reputation of the institution; increase college-admission standards; spend more money on academic, co-curricular, and extracurricular programs; and improve retention and graduation rates.

The value added by college rankings, though prestigious, is limited by several dynamics, such as disregard for institutional mission, failure to consider such student-level factors as family household income and first-generation status, and data integrity challenges. While it is not impossible to improve institutional rankings, postsecondary institutions should not become distracted from critical student-centered agendas because of overemphasis on college rankings.

REFERENCES

Alstyne, S. (1982). Ranking the law schools: The reality of illusion? *Law & Social Inquiry, 7*(3), 649–684.

Bardaro, K. (2012, June 21). Addressing critics of the PayScale college ROI rankings. *PayScale*. Retrieved from https://www.payscale.com/career-news/2012/06/college-roi-critics.

Carey, K. (2006, September). College rankings reformed: The case for a new order in higher education. *Education Sector*. Retrieved from https://www.issuelab.org/resources/533/533.pdf.

Collins, H. W., Jenkins, S. M., Strzelecka, N., Gasman, M., Wang, N., & Nguyen, T. H. (2014). Ranking and rewarding access: An alternative college scorecard. *Penn Center for Minority Serving Institutions*. Retrieved from https://www.gse.upenn.edu/pdf/cmsi/alternative_college_scorecard.pdf.

Diver, C. (2005). Is there life after rankings? *Atlantic Monthly, 296*(4), 136.

Espinosa, L. L., Crandall, J. R., & Tukibayeva, M. (2014, March). Rankings, institutional behavior, and college and university choice: Framing the national dialogue on Obama's ratings plan. *American Council on Education*. Retrieved from https://www.acenet.edu/news-room/Documents/Rankings-Institutional-Behavior-and-College-and-University-Choice.pdf.

Finder, A. (2007, June 20). Some colleges to drop out of *U.S. News* rankings. *New York Times*.

Gnolek, S. L., Falciano, V. T., & Kuncl, R. W. (2014). Modeling change and variation in *U.S. News & World Report* college rankings: What would it really take to be in the top 20? *Research in Higher Education, 55*(8), 761–779.

Goglio, V. (2016). One size fits all? A different perspective on university rankings. *Journal of Higher Education Policy and Management, 38*(2), 212–226.

Hazelkorn, E. (2015). *Rankings and the reshaping of higher education: The battle for world-class excellence.* 2nd ed. Basingstoke, UK: Palgrave Macmillan.

Huntington-Klein, N. (2016). *The search: The effect of the College Scorecard on interest in colleges*. Unpublished manuscript.

Jaschik, S. (2018, February 19). 3 more instances of false data in 'U.S. News' rankings. *Inside Higher Ed*. Retrieved from https://www.insidehighered.com/admissions/article/2018/02/19/false-us-news-rankings-data-discovered-three-more-universities.

Jones, W. A. (2016). Do college rankings matter? Examining the influence of "America's best black colleges" on HBCU undergraduate admissions. *American Journal of Education*, *122*(2), 247–265.

Jöns, H., & Hoyler, M. (2013). Global geographies of higher education: The perspective of world university rankings. *Geoforum*, *46*, 45–59.

Kim, J. (2018, February). The functions and dysfunctions of college rankings: An analysis of institutional expenditure. *Research in Higher Education*, *58*(1), 54–87.

Klein, M. W. (2015, March). What counts: The policy and politics of the proposed college rating system in the United States. *Higher Education Forum: A COE Publication*, *12*, 57–76.

Kulkarni, S., & Rothwell, J. (2015, April 29). Beyond college rankings: A value-added approach to assessing two- and four-year schools. *Brookings*. Retrieved from https://www.brookings.edu/research/beyond-college-rankings-a-value-added-approach-to-assessing-two-and-four-year-schools/.

Lederman, D. (2017, April 18). PayScale's impact (and limitations). *Inside Higher Ed*. Retrieved from https://www.insidehighered.com/news/2017/04/18/payscale-rankings-roi-have-influence-and-significant-limitations.

Lockwood, R., & Hadd, J. (2007). Building a brand in higher education. *Business Journal*. Retrieved from http://www.gallup.com/businessjournal/28081/Building-Brand-Higher-Education.aspx.

Machung, A. (1998). Playing the ranking game. *Change: The Magazine of Higher Learning*, *30*(4), 12–16.

Maclean, A. H. H. (1900). *Where we get our best men: Some statistics showing their nationalities, counties, towns, schools, universities, and other antecedents: 1837–1897*. London.

Magoun, H. W. (1966). The Cartter Report on quality in graduate education: Institutional and divisional standings compiled from the report. *Journal of Higher Education*, *37*(9), 481–492.

Martin, J. P. (2015). Moving up in the *US News and World Report* rankings. *Change: The Magazine of Higher Learning*, *47*(2), 52–61.

Morse, R., Brooks, E., & Mason, M. (2015). How *U.S. News* calculated the 2016 best colleges rankings. *U.S. News & World Report*. Retrieved from http://uair.arizona.edu/sites/uair/files/uafiles/IR/Rankings/usnwr_2016_ug_methodology.pdf.

Myers, L., & Robe, J. (2009, March). College rankings: History, criticism and reform. *Center for College Affordability and Productivity*. Retrieved from https://files.eric.ed.gov/fulltext/ED536277.pdf.

Sanoff, A. P. (2007, April). The *US News* college rankings: A view from the inside. In Institute for Higher Education Policy (Ed.), *College and university ranking systems: Global perspectives and American challenges* (pp. 9–21). Washington, DC: Institute for Higher Education Policy.

Smith, P. (2012). Ranking and the globalization of higher education. *Silpakorn University Journal of Social Sciences, Humanities, and Arts*, *12*(2), 35–70.

Stewart, J. B. (2013, September 13). New metric for colleges: Graduates' salaries. *New York Times*, p. 13.

Stewart, J. B. (2015, October 15). College rankings fail to measure the influence of the institution. *New York Times*, October 15, 2015.

Stuart, D. L. (1995). Reputational rankings: Background and development. *New Directions for Institutional Research*, *1995*(88), 13–20.

Tierney, J. (2013, September 10). Your annual reminder to ignore the *US News & World Report* college rankings. *Atlantic*.

Webster, D. S. (1986). *Academic quality rankings of American colleges and universities*. Springfield, IL: Charles C. Thomas.

Whitehurst, G. J., & Chingos, M. M. (2015). Deconstructing and reconstructing the College Scorecard. *Evidence Speaks Report, 1*(4).

Wills, C. E. (2016, November). Impact of STEM focus on graduation rates in ranking colleges. *Computer Science Department, Worcester Polytechnic Institute.* Retrieved from http://web. cs.wpi.edu/~cew/papers/stem16.pdf.

Chapter Four

College Attrition and the "Value-Added" Proposition

There are many proven benefits of college matriculation, including employment and career opportunities, increased wages and benefits, the development of cognitive and noncognitive skills, social and civic engagement, and career preparation. The College Board's report *Education Pays 2016: The Benefits of Higher Education for Individuals and Society* states,

> As the wealth of data . . . shows, the average payoff of higher education is very high. Earning a bachelor's degree or a graduate degree leads to the highest earnings, the lowest unemployment rates, the widest range of career opportunities, and the sharpest differences in civic participation and health related behaviors such as smoking and exercise. (Ma, Pender, & Welch, 2016, p. 7)

A 2013 study by Gallup and the Lumina Foundation found that Americans, both with and without earned degrees, still believe in the importance of postsecondary education, with more than 9 in 10 (94 percent) saying a postsecondary degree or credential is at least somewhat important and 70 percent saying it is very important (Calderon & Sorenson, 2014) (see figure 4.1).

IT'S NOT JUST MONEY

A 72-page Lumina Foundation issue paper "It's Not Just Money: The Benefit of College Education to Individuals and Society" (Trostel, 2015) suggests that there are both "private benefits" of college education (those that accrue to the individuals obtaining the degree and their families) and "external" or "spillover" benefits (benefits that accrue to the rest of society). Philip Trostel summarizes the benefits for Americans with bachelor's degrees (and without

Importance of Postsecondary Degree

How important is having a certificate or degree beyond high school?

	% U.S. adults	% With high school diploma or less	% With some college	% With college degree or certificate
Very important	70	66	60	77
Somewhat important	24	26	33	20
Not very important	4	5	3	3
Not at all important	1	1	3	<0.5

Source: 2013 Gallup-Lumina Foundation Poll on Higher Education

GALLUP

Figure 4.1.   Results from a study by Gallup and the Lumina Foundation with a random sample of US adults, November 25 to December 15, 2013.

graduate degrees) in comparison to high school graduates never attending college:

- Annual earnings are about $32,000 (134 percent) higher. Moreover, there is no evidence that the college earnings premium is declining. Indeed, it has been increasing.
- Lifetime earnings are, conservatively, about $625,000 (114 percent) greater in present discounted value (using a 3 percent real interest rate and taking forgone earnings while in college into account).
- The incidence of poverty is 3.5 times lower.
- The likelihood of having health insurance through employment is 47 percent higher. Annual additional compensation in the form of employer contributions for health insurance is $1,400 (74 percent greater).
- The likelihood of having a retirement plan through employment is 72 percent greater. Retirement income is 2.4 times higher.
- Job safety is greater. The incidence of receiving workers' compensation is 2.4 times lower.
- Measures of occupational prestige are significantly higher.
- The probability of being employed is 24 percent higher.
- The likelihood of being unemployed is 2.2 times lower.
- The likelihood of being out of the labor force (neither employed nor unemployed) is 74 percent lower.
- Age at retirement is higher. The probability of being retired between the ages 62 through 69 is about 25 percent lower.
- The likelihood of reporting health to be very good or excellent is 44 percent higher.
- The likelihood of being a regular smoker is 3.9 times lower. The incidence of obesity and heavy drinking are significantly lower. The likelihood of

exercising, having a healthy diet, wearing seat belts, and seeking preventative medical care are significantly higher.
- The incidence of a disability making it difficult to live independently is 3.6 times lower.
- Life expectancy at age 25 is seven years longer (for those having at least some college compared to those never having gone to college).
- Asset income is 4.9 times greater ($1,900 more per year).
- The likelihood of not having a bank account is 8.1 times lower. Reliance on expensive forms of banking and credit is significantly lower.
- The probability of being in prison or jail is 4.9 times lower.
- The probability of being married is 21 percent higher and the probability of being divorced or separated is 61 percent lower.
- The likelihood of being happy is significantly higher. (pp. 1–2)

Trostel further summarizes the benefits that the rest of society receives from those with bachelor's degrees (and without graduate degrees) in comparison to high school graduates never attending college:

- Although the evidence is not completely conclusive, the positive effect on the aggregate earnings of others appears to be roughly similar to the effect on own earnings.
- Lifetime taxes are, conservatively, $273,000 (215 percent) greater in present discounted value (using a 3 percent real interest rate and taking into account forgone taxes while in college). That is, college graduates contribute hundreds of thousands of dollars more toward government services and social insurance programs.
- Lifetime government expenditures are about $81,000 (39 percent) lower in present value. College graduates rely much less on other taxpayers.
- The lifetime total fiscal effect is roughly $355,000 in present value.
- Crime is significantly lower.
- Volunteering is 2.3 times more likely. The estimated value of volunteer labor is 4.1 times ($1,300 annually) greater.
- Employment in the nonprofit sector is twice as likely. The estimated value of the implicit wage contribution to nonprofits is 8.7 times ($1,500 annually) greater.
- Annual cash donations to charities are $900 (3.4 times) higher.
- Total philanthropic contributions (i.e., the value of volunteer labor plus the value of the implicit contribution to nonprofits plus cash donations) are $3,600 (4.7 times) higher.
- Voting and political involvement are significantly higher.
- Participation in school, community, service, civic, and religious organizations is substantially (1.9 times) higher. Leadership in these organizations is particularly (3.2 times) greater.
- Community involvement is significantly greater. For example, attendance at community meetings is 2.6 times greater.
- Neighborhood interactions and trust are significantly higher. (pp. 2–3)

The Lumina Foundation report provides overwhelming evidence that invest-ment in college education adds exponential value, both for individuals and for society. Trostel argues that the typically emphasized financial payoff of postsecondary education is only the tip of the "college-payoff iceberg," where many more benefits to college education are hidden beneath the sur-face than are displayed above the surface.

RETURN ON INVESTMENT:
MORE MONEY, MORE MONEY, MORE MONEY

Abel and Deitz (2014) observe, "By the end of 2013, aggregate student loan debt in the United States exceeded $1 trillion, and more than 11 percent of student loan balances were either severely delinquent or already in default. With the costs of college rising and the benefits in doubt, many are wonder-ing whether earning a college degree still pays" (p. 1). While it might seem as if the value of a college degree has declined because of falling wages and rising tuition, Abel and Deitz argue that this is actually not the case. Instead, after climbing impressively between 1980 and 2000, the return on a college degree has held steady at around 15 percent, well surpassing the threshold for a sound investment. In fact, Greenstone and Looney (2011) conclude that higher education is a much better investment than almost any other alterna-tive, with the benefits of a four-year college degree being equivalent to an investment that returns 15.2 percent per year, more than double the average return on stock market investments since 1950 and more than five times the returns on corporate bonds, gold, long-term government bonds, or home ownership; from any investment perspective, college is a great deal (see figure 4.2).

Abel and Deitz conclude that the driving force behind the steady or in-creasing return on investment for college graduates is that the wages of those without a college degree also have been falling, keeping the college-wage premium near an all-time high while reducing the opportunity cost of going to school. Abel and Deitz define the *opportunity cost* of a college education as the value of what someone must give up to attend college, which typically is equivalent to the wages that could have been earned by working instead of going to college. Even though the new millennium has been a challenging period for college graduates by some measures, those with less education have struggled even more (see figure 4.3).

Pew Research Center shows that the median adjusted monthly household income of households headed by people with postsecondary education be-tween ages 25 and 34 increased over a 25-year period, with further increases at the bachelor's, master's, and doctoral levels of degree attainment (Fry, 2014). For young people with bachelor's degrees heading households,

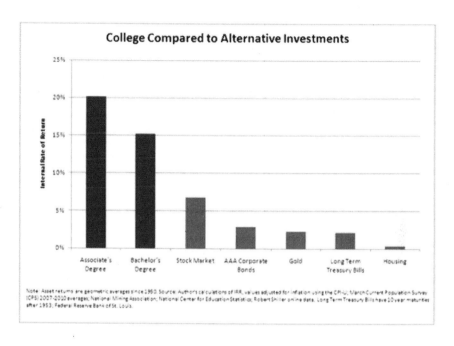

Figure 4.2.　*Source:* Greenstone & Looney (2011).

monthly income has increased by 15 percent in 25 years, from $5,960 in 1984 to $7,232 in 2009. Meanwhile, for young people heading households with only a high school diploma, monthly income has decreased by 15 percent in 25 years, from $3,587 in 1984 to $3,067 in 2009 (see figure 4.4). This data provides more evidence of a significant financial pay-off for college graduates, even at a young age.

WHAT ABOUT MILLENNIALS? IS COLLEGE PAYING OFF FOR THEM, TOO?

A 2013 Pew Research Center report on higher education details how college-educated millennials have been outperforming their less-educated peers on virtually every economic measure, and the gap between the two groups has only grown over time. For late baby boomers in 1986, the difference between the earnings of a high school graduate ($30,525) and a graduate of a four-year college ($44,770) was only $14,245. For millennials in 2013, though, the difference between the earnings of a high school graduate ($28,000) and graduate a of a four-year college ($45,500) was $17,500. This is a 19 percent increase. in the difference between high school graduates and four-year col-

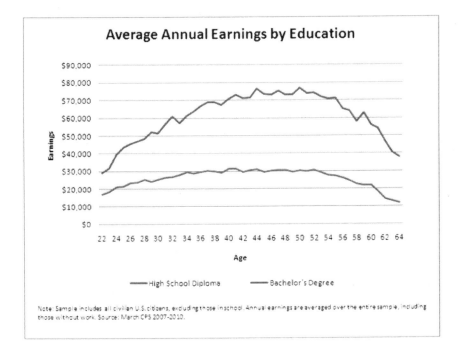

Figure 4.3.   *Source:* Greenstone & Looney (2011).

lege graduates in the median annual earnings of full-time workers ages 25 to 32.

Not only are millennial college graduates earning more money than their counterparts with a high school diploma, two-year degree, or some college, but also they are less likely to be unemployed, less likely to live in poverty, less likely to live in their parents' homes, and more likely to be married (see figure 4.6). Despite the common perception, millennials continue to benefit greatly from obtaining a college education.

MILLENNIALS: *VALUE ADDED* MEANS "OPPORTUNITY"

Serving as both the director of student success and retention and the associate chief university marshal has afforded me the opportunity to observe students on the first day of new student orientation, when they enter the university as freshmen, and when they leave the university as new graduates on commencement day. I often notice a visible change in students' appearance after their four to six years of matriculation. A maturity and vibe of optimism and expectancy radiate from students as they leave the university,

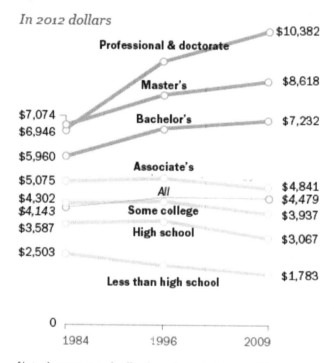

Median Adjusted Monthly Household Income of Households Headed by 25- to 34-Year-Olds

In 2012 dollars

Professional & doctorate — $10,382

Master's — $8,618

$7,074
$6,946

Bachelor's — $7,232

$5,960

Associate's

$5,075

All

$4,302
$4,143

Some college

$3,587

High school

$2,503

$4,841
$4,479
$3,937

$3,067

Less than high school — $1,783

0

1984   1996   2009

Note: Income standardized to a household size of three.

Source: Pew Research Center tabulations of the 1984, 1996 and 2009 Survey of Income and Program Participation (SIPP) Education and Training History topical module.

PEW RESEARCH CENTER

Figure 4.4.

ready to face the challenges of new careers, graduate school, volunteerism, raising families, and civic engagement. Their demeanor as seniors is a far cry from the awkward, tentative, and sometimes fearful dispositions during their new-student orientation week.

It seems as if some level of transformation has taken place in the lives of students who pass through the hallowed halls of our nation's institutions of

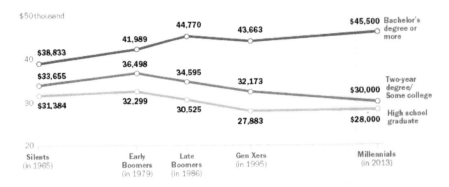

Median annual earnings among full-time workers ages 25 to 32, in 2012 dollars

Source: Pew Research Center tabulations of the 2013, 1995, 1986, 1979 and 1965 March Current Population Survey (CPS) IPUMS

PEW RESEARCH CENTER

Figure 4.5.

higher learning, transformations that have the potential to pay off both liter-
ally and figuratively over their lifetimes. I am always honored when recent
graduates stop by my office to share their success stories with me. The most
unlikely of our students, the students whom I didn't necessarily observe any
outward signs of transformation from their first day of orientation to their
last day at commencement, are the ones that shock and thrill me the most.
Several students exude this exit maturity, two of whom are worthy of men-
tioning.

Both students were black males who at some time worked for the Office of
Student Success and Retention in the role of peer mentor or office assistant,
and both were students who performed borderline academically, but we de-
cided to give them an opportunity to serve as peer mentors in spite of their
lackluster academic performances. Both had graduated from college with
GPAs in the 2.5 range, with "thank-you-Lordy" honors; one was from Balti-
more, and the other from Chicago. The first young man, Lateef, wrote to me
from Afghanistan to request a recommendation for his promotion from SPC
(specialist) in the US Army to officer at the age of 26. Lateef was never in our
Army ROTC program, nor did he ever express any interest in ROTC or a
career in the miltary during college. He attached photos of himself in Af-
ghanistan looking so mature and clean-cut that he was almost unrecogniz-
able.

He later visited my office to thank me for the letter of recommendation
and to confirm that he had earned the promotion, a promotion he was only

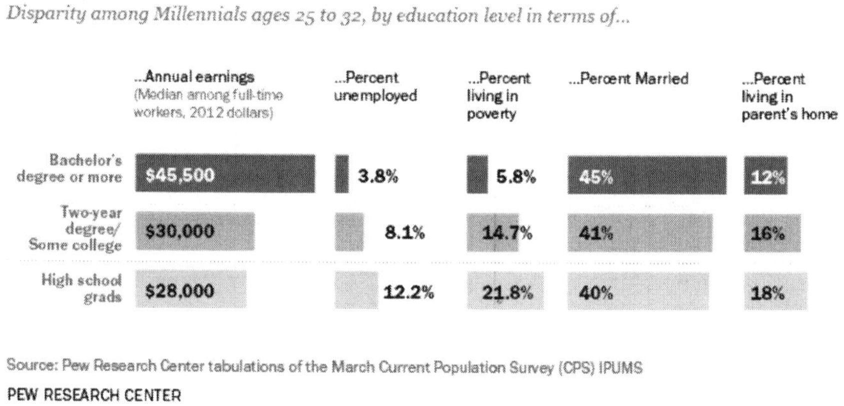

Disparity among Millennials ages 25 to 32, by education level in terms of...

	...Annual earnings (Median among full-time workers, 2012 dollars)	...Percent unemployed	...Percent living in poverty	...Percent Married	...Percent living in parent's home
Bachelor's degree or more	$45,500	3.8%	5.8%	45%	12%
Two-year degree/ Some college	$30,000	8.1%	14.7%	41%	16%
High school grads	$28,000	12.2%	21.8%	40%	18%

Source: Pew Research Center tabulations of the March Current Population Survey (CPS) IPUMS
PEW RESEARCH CENTER

Figure 4.6.

eligible for because he was a college graduate. The other student, Jonathan, returned to my office last year on Career Day, wearing a suit and tie; he was a recruiter for a tech company in Arlington, VA. He also had been promoted in his 20s after working for his company for two years. He, too, shared with me that he was only eligible for his promotion because of his college degree, even though there were people who had been at the company longer but had never completed their degrees.

I personally have engaged with thousands of young African American men and women who, without the benefit of their college degrees, would not have been employed in professional careers and would not have earned promotions in those careers. Many of these students are in the millennial generation, a generation some higher-education professionals have written off but who still benefit greatly from earning degrees or advanced credentials in higher education.

IMPACT OF THE GREAT RECESSION

In reference to America's recovery since the Great Recession, the Georgetown University Center on Education and the Workforce's *America's Divided Recovery: College Haves and Have-Nots* report deliniates,

- Nearly all the jobs created in the recovery, 11.5 million out of 11.6 million, have gone to workers with at least some postsecondary education (see figure 4.8).

Percent of college graduates in each generation who say that considering what they and their family paid for their undergraduate education, it ...

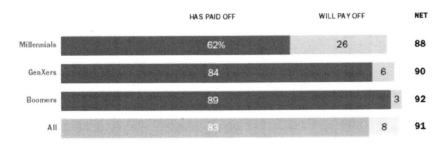

Source: Pew Research Center survey, Oct. 7-27, 2013, N=2,002
PEW RESEARCH CENTER

Figure 4.7.

- Workers with at least some postsecondary education have also captured the vast majority of the good jobs—jobs that pay more than $53,000 per year for full-time, full-year workers and come with benefits.
- At the other end of the education spectrum, workers with a high school diploma or less essentially have experienced no job recovery.
- For the first time, workers with a bachelor's degree or higher make up a larger proportion of the workforce (36 percent) than workers with a high school diploma or less (34 percent).
- Workers with a high school diploma or less are losing access to high-skill and middle-skill jobs and increasingly are settling for low-skill, low-wage jobs (Carnevale, Jayasundera, & Gulish, 2016).

The Georgetown report also points out that those with the most years of college were the last fired in the recession and the first hired in the recovery. Further, the report warns that, while men without a college degree were traditionally able to make their way into the middle class through manufacturing and construction jobs and women without a college degree could get middle-class jobs in office- and administrative-support occupations, as these pathways increasingly close down, few opportunities remain to advance to the middle class without postsecondary education.

DO COLLEGE GRADUATES LIVE BETTER LIVES?

One of the reasons many Americans still value higher education is the belief that earning postsecondary credentials expands career opportunities and im-

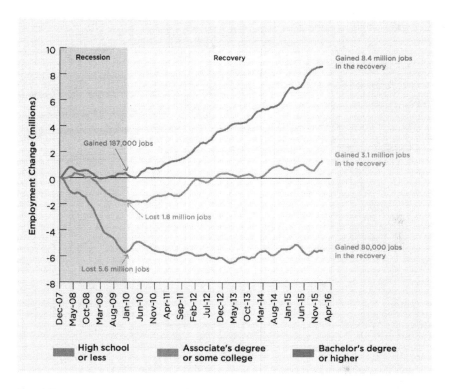

Source: Georgetown University Center on Education and the Workforce analysis of *Current Population Survey* (CPS) data, 2007-2016.
Note: Employment includes all workers age 18 and older. The monthly employment numbers are seasonally adjusted using the U.S. Census Bureau X-12 procedure and smoothed using a four-month moving average.

Figure 4.8. In the recovery, there have been an added 8.4 million jobs for workers with a bachelor's degree but only 80,000 jobs (after losing 5.6 million jobs in the recession) for workers with a high school diploma or less. *Source:* Carnevale, Jayasundera, & Gulish (2016).

proves the standard of living. According to Gallup, nearly three in four Americans (73 percent) agree or strongly agree that having a certificate, certification, or degree beyond high school is essential for getting a good job, and most US adults (74 percent) see a postsecondary degree or credential as a pathway to a better quality of life (Gallup & Purdue University, 2014) (see figures 4.9 and 4.10).

College education is associated with increased life expectancy, healthier lifestyles, and reducing health-care costs. Ma, Pender, and Welch (2016) report that adults with higher levels of education are more active citizens than others and are more involved in their children's activities:

Postsecondary Degree Essential for a Good Job and a Better Life

On a five-point scale, where 5 means strongly agree and 1 means strongly disagree, please indicate your level of agreement with each of the following statements about higher education and the workforce.

	% 1 Strongly disagree	% 2	% 3	% 4	% 5 Strongly agree
Certificate, certification, or degree beyond high school is essential for getting a good job	5	6	16	29	44
Postsecondary degree or credential leads to a better quality of life	3	6	17	34	40

Source: 2013 Gallup-Lumina Foundation Poll on Higher Education

GALLUP

Figure 4.9.

- In 2014, 69 percent of 25- to 34-year-olds with at least a bachelor's degree and 45 percent of high school graduates reported exercising vigorously at least once a week.
- Children of parents with higher levels of educational attainment are more likely than others to engage in a variety of educational activities with their family members.
- Among adults age 25 and older, 16 percent of those with a high school diploma volunteered in 2015, compared with 39 percent of those with at least a bachelor's degree.
- In the 2014 midterm election, the voting rate of 25- to 44-year-olds with at least a bachelor's degree (45 percent) was more than twice as high as the voting rate of high school graduates (20 percent) in the same age group. (p. 4)

According to the 2014 Gallup and Purdue University study of more than 30,000 college graduates across the United States, nearly 9 in 10 graduates say they are satisfied with their lives and, on average, rate their current lives a 7.4 on a 10-point scale, where 10 is the best possible life. Gallup reports that people's evaluations of their current lives rise with education, with college graduates and those with postgraduate education giving their lives the highest ratings.

College education increases the likelihood of adults moving up the socioeconomic ladder and reduces the likelihood of adults relying on public assistance (Ma, Pender, & Welch, 2016). *Education Pays* (2016) states that among high school sophomores whose parents were in the lowest income group in 2001, 21 percent of those who earned at least a bachelor's degree,

17 percent of those with an associate degree, and 13 percent of those with only a high school diploma had reached the highest income quartile themselves 10 years later.

HEALTH BENEFITS OF COLLEGE EDUCATION

Although life expectancy for men (76 years) and women (81 years) has risen to record highs in the United States, disparities along education lines persist; the remaining life expectancy at age 25 is about a decade shorter for people who do not have a high school degree compared with those who have completed college (National Center for Health Statistics, 2012). According to the National Center for Health Statistics (NCHS), parental education and income may be related to both high educational attainment and longevity among US adults. In fact, highly educated adults in the United States have lower yearly mortality rates than less-educated people across all age, gender, and racial and ethnic subgroups. A 2011 study over a 16-year period found that women ages 25 to 44 with 9 to 11 years of education had a 202 percent higher mortality rate than similarly aged women who had completed at least 17 years of education (see figure 4.11). The NCHS reports that, from 2007 to 2010, 39 percent of women who were high school graduates or had a GED were obese, compared to 25 percent of women who had earned a bachelor's degree or higher, a difference of 14 percent. For men, 37 percent of high school graduates or those with GEDs were obese, compared to 28 percent of men who had earned a bachelor's degree or higher, a difference of 9 percent (see figure 4.12). The NCHS reports that, from 2007 to 2010, obesity among children ages 2 to 19 years old in households with parents who had a high

Percent of employed adults ages 25 to 32 with each level of education saying...

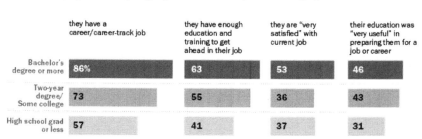

Source: Pew Research Center survey, Oct. 7-27, 2013, N=2,002
PEW RESEARCH CENTER

Figure 4.10.

school diploma or GED was 19 percent for boys and 21 percent for girls; obesity among children in households with parents who had a bachelor's degree or higher was 11 percent for boys and 7 percent for girls, a difference of 8 percent for boys and 14 percent for girls (see figure 4.13). For people ages 25 to 64 years between the years 2000 and 2010, smoking was more than 30 percent for high school graduates or people with a GED, compared to less than 10 percent for people with a bachelor's degree or higher, a difference of more than 20 percent (see figure 4.14). While the incidence of smoking has decreased in general from 2000 to 2010, gaps by education level persist at all ages.

Ross and Mirowsky (2010) found that depression decreased more steeply for women than for men as the level of education increased, while the gender gap in depression essentially disappeared among persons with a college degree or higher. The associations between education level and mortality and such health outcomes as obesity, smoking, and depression are likely due to well-informed reasoning about the risk of disease, as well as the adoption of prevention strategies over a lifetime as a result of higher education (Baker, Leon, Smith Greenaway, Collins, & Movit, 2011). Prevention strategies include vigorous exercise; only 40 percent of high school graduates report engaging in vigorous exercise at least once per week, compared to 68 percent of four-year-college graduates (Baum, Ma, & Payea, 2010).

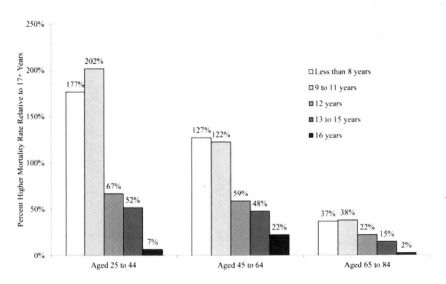

Source: Robert A. Hummer and Joseph T. Lariscy, "Educational Attainment and Adult Mortality," in *International Handbook of Adult Mortality*, ed. Richard G. Rogers and Eileen M. Crimmins (NY: Springer, 2011)

Figure 4.11. Mortality rates of women by years of education.

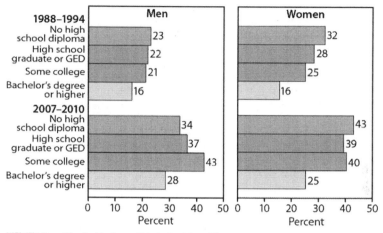

Figure 4.12.

HEALTH BENEFITS: UP CLOSE AND PERSONAL

My academic discipline is public health. As a health educator, I had the privilege of teaching two courses per semester for 18 consecutive semesters at Morgan State University (MSU), a public, urban, historically black university in Maryland. Each semester, I instructed about 60 undergraduates, primarily African American students, many of whom were first-generation college students.

I was shocked to find out how little information many of my students had for their personal health, especially after 12 or more years of formal education. Thus, it is absolutely no surprise to me that people who complete college are less likely to be obese, to smoke, and to drink heavily and more likely to eat nutritious meals and wear their seat belts. These are health behaviors that were covered in my health class, "Healthful Living," a required course for all undergraduate students at MSU. Assignments included completing the "My Pyramid/My Plate" at www.health.gov, which requires students to outline their family health history through a family tree, and keeping a detailed food journal for three full days. This assignment revealed to my students a number of challenges facing them in their own personal health journeys.

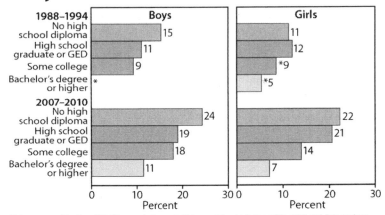

Obesity among children 2–19 years, by education level of household head

*Estimates are considered unreliable. Data preceded by an asterisk have a relative standard error (RSE) of 20%–30%. Data not shown have an RSE of greater than 30%.
NOTES: GED is General Educational Development high school equivalency diploma. Obesity is body mass index at or above the sex- and age-specific 95th percentile from the 2000 CDC Growth Charts.
SOURCE: CDC/NCHS, *Health, United States, 2011*, Figure 25. Data from the National Health and Nutrition Examination Survey.

Figure 4.13.

Many of my students interviewed their grandparents and parents to get a better idea of their family health history, only to find out that there were underlying chronic illnesses in their family, of which they had no knowledge, such as diabetes, hypertension, bipolar disorder, and addiction. We discussed the importance of early detection and frequent health screenings. I gave my students extra credit for attending the Health Expo in Baltimore and other special health-related events.

Several of my students experienced extreme weight loss, some more than 100 pounds, after learning in my class much more about nutrition, a balanced diet, and exercise. One student came back several years after her graduation from college to thank me for the information she learned in health class, and I didn't even recognize her because she had lost so much weight by changing her entire lifestyle.

Additionally, I required my students to write a final paper about how they planned to make lifestyle changes based on what they had learned in the course. Many students expressed the desire to cut back on such behaviors as drinking, smoking, and overeating, while others challenged themselves to become proactive by exercising regularly, buying a scale to weigh themselves more frequently, and—one of my personal favorites—eating more fiber and drinking more water daily. I do not believe that my health class was

Current cigarette smoking

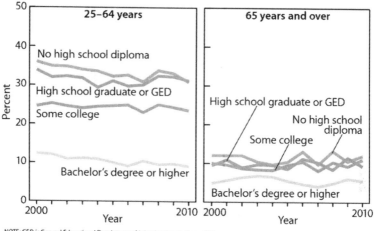

NOTE: GED is General Educational Development high school equivalency diploma.
SOURCE: CDC/NCHS, *Health, United States, 2011*, Figure 38. Data from the National Health Interview Survey.

Figure 4.14.

exceptional but rather that it represented a typical postsecondary level learning experience in the field of health education, a learning laboratory that has the potential to be life-changing.

WHAT IS IT ABOUT COLLEGE
THAT PROMOTES THESE BENEFITS?

Based on research conducted on college teaching and learning, good practice in undergraduate education (1) encourages contacts between students and faculty, (2) develops reciprocity and cooperation among students, (3) uses active-learning techniques, (4) gives prompt feedback, (5) emphasizes time on task, (6) communicates high expectations, and (7) respects diverse talents and ways of learning (Chickering & Gamson, 1987). Results from the Gallup and Purdue University (2014) study confirm that, if graduates have (1) a professor who cares about them as people, (2) makes them excited about learning, and (3) encourages them to pursue their dreams, then their odds of being engaged at work more than double, as do their odds of thriving. The study also notes that, if graduates had (4) an internship or job where they were able to apply what they were learning in the classroom, (5) were actively involved in extracurricular activities and organizations, and (6) worked on projects that took a semester or more to complete, then their odds of being engaged at work doubled.

The seven best practices presented by Chickering and Gamson (1987) and the six elements of the college experience presented in the Gallup and Purdue University (2014) study show how college students feeling supported and having meaningful and engaging learning experiences can lead to long-term success for college graduates. Trostel (2015) concludes, "In its purest form, traditional college education teaches critical thinking, self-examination and open-mindedness; it encourages exploration into new ways of understanding and cultivates creativity, innovation, tolerance, inclusivity and diversity" (p. 67).

Some of the benefits of the college experience can be attributed to those who attend college but do not graduate. For example, those who enroll in a two- or four-year program but do not attain a degree also experience substantial increases in earnings. On average, students who attended college but did not finish made about $8,000 per year more than those with just a high school diploma; over a lifetime, this results in more than $100,000 in earnings (Greenstone & Looney, 2013). Importantly, there are inherent benefits of attending and participating in the overall college experience for all students, regardless of degree completion. Of course, the financial benefits of higher education are most obvious, but the opportunities that college education affords, the values that college education promotes, and the soft skills and life skills that influence health and life satisfaction add value to the human experience.

THE BOTTOM LINE

The benefits of earning a college degree are undeniable; college graduates are less likely to be unemployed and more likely to own a home. College graduates earn more money, live healthier lifestyles, have longer life expectancies, report greater satisfaction levels, and claim higher quality of life. Notwithstanding the rising cost of tuition and falling wages, the return on investment for college education is holding steady at 15 percent, outpacing the threshold for a sound financial investment (Abel & Deitz, 2014). Despite the Great Recession, college education remains the most proven, invaluable, lifetime investment and serves as the most reliable path to upward mobility and socioeconomic class reassignment.

REFERENCES

Abel, J. R., & Deitz, R. (2014). Do the benefits of college still outweigh the costs? *Current Issues in Economics and Finance, 20*(3).

Baker, D. P., Leon, J., Smith Greenaway, E. G., Collins, J., & Movit, M. (2011). The education effect on population health: A reassessment. *Population and Development Review, 37*(2), 307–332.

Baum, S., Ma, J., & Payea, K. (2010). Education pays, 2010: The benefits of higher education for individuals and society. Trends in Higher Education Series. *College Board Advocacy & Policy Center.* Retrieved from https://trends.collegeboard.org/sites/default/files/education-pays-2010-full-report.pdf.

Calderon, V. J., & Sorenson, S. (2014, April 7). Americans say college degree leads to a better life. *Gallup.* Retrieved from https://news.gallup.com/poll/168386/americans-say-college-degree-leads-better-life.aspx.

Carnevale, A. P., Jayasundera, T., & Gulish, A. (2016, June). America's divided recovery: College haves and have-nots. *Georgetown University Center on Education and the Workforce.* Retrieved from https://cew.georgetown.edu/wp-content/uploads/Americas-Divided-Recovery-web.pdf.

Chickering, A. W., & Gamson, Z. F. (1987). Seven principles for good practice in undergraduate education. *AAHE Bulletin, 3,* 7.

Fry, R. (2014, February 28). For millennials, a bachelor's degree continues to pay off, but a master's earns even more. *Pew Research Center.* Retrieved from http://pewrsr.ch/1fO4t1p.

Gallup & Purdue University. (2014). Great jobs great lives: The 2014 Gallup–Purdue index report. *Gallup.* Retrieved from https://news.gallup.com/reports/197141/gallup-purdue-index-report-2014.aspx.

Greenstone, M., & Looney, A. (2011, June 25). Where is the best place to invest $102,000: In stocks, bonds, or a college degree? *Brookings.* Retrieved from: https://www.brookings.edu/research/where-is-the-best-place-to-invest-102000-in-stocks-bonds-or-a-college-degree/.

Greenstone, M., & Looney, A. (2013, June 6). Is starting college and not finishing really that bad? *Hamilton Project.* Retrieved from http://www.hamiltonproject.org/papers/what_happens_to_students_who_fail_to_complete_a_college_degree_is_some.

Ma, J., Pender, M., & Welch, M. (2016). Education pays 2016: The benefits of higher education for individuals and society. *College Board.* Retrieved from https://trends.collegeboard.org/sites/default/files/education-pays-2016-full-report.pdf.

National Center for Health Statistics. (2012). *Health, United States, 2011: With special feature on socioeconomic status and health.* Hyattsville, MD: US Department of Health and Human Services. Retrieved from https://www.cdc.gov/nchs/data/hus/hus11.pdf.

Ross, C. E., & Mirowsky, J. (2010). Why education is the key to socioeconomic differentials in health. In C. E. Bird, P. Conrad, A. M. Fremont, & S. Timmermans (Eds.), *Handbook of medical sociology,* 6th ed. (pp. 33–51). Nashville: Vanderbilt University Press.

Trostel, P. (2015, October 14). It's not just the money: the benefits of college education to individuals and to society. *Lumina Foundation.* Retrieved from https://www.luminafoundation.org/files/resources/its-not-just-the-money.pdf.

Chapter Five

HBCUs, MSIs, and the College Completion Game

Some researchers have suggested that the only way to achieve the college completion goals set forth by the Obama administration, Complete College America, the Lumina Foundation, and other national stakeholders is to focus on underserved students who are the fastest-growing demographic in the Unites States but whose rates of college attainment are the lowest (Harmon, 2012). The postsecondary institutions primarily serving these students are the nation's historically black colleges and universities (HBCUs) and minority-serving institutions (MSIs).

WHAT ARE HBCUs AND MSIs?

According to the White House Initiative on HBCUs, HBCUs are institutions established prior to 1964, whose principal mission is the education of black Americans. Most of the 105 HBCUs are 4-year institutions and represent a diverse array in 19 states, the District of Columbia, and the Virgin Islands.

In 1862, the first land-grant college provisions, known as the First Morrill Act, were enacted by the US Congress. Morrill Act funds were distributed to the states in the late 1860s with the intention of fostering educational opportunity for all students, especially newly freed blacks (Provasnik & Shafer, 2004). In 1890, the US Congress passed the Second Morrill Act, requiring states with dual systems of higher education for all-white and nonwhite institutions to provide land grants for both systems; 19 agricultural, mechanical, and industrial land-grant institutions for blacks were organized and designated as HBCUs.

Minority-serving institutions are eligible for the federal designation as result of meeting the criteria outlined in Titles III, IV, and V of the Higher Education Act and include two- and four-year colleges and universities that are HBCUs, Hispanic-serving institutions (HSIs), tribal colleges and universities (TCUs), Alaska native– and native Hawaiian–serving institutions (ANNHs), Native American–serving nontribal institutions (NASNTIs), predominantly black institutions (PBIs), and Asian American– and Native American Pacific Islander–serving institutions (AANAPISIs). According to 2014 National Center for Education Statistics IPEDS data, MSIs make up about a third of all undergraduate institutions nationally and enroll more than half of all minority students.

GAPS IN GRADUATION RATES BY RACE AND ETHNICITY

In 2009, the US Census Bureau reported that only 27.4 percent of the adult population in the United States had completed college, with just 19 percent of African Americans and 12 percent of Hispanics (of any race) between the ages of 25 and 29 having earned a college degree, compared to 37 percent of whites in this age group (DeAngelo, Franke, Hurtado, Pryor, & Tran, 2011). There are many possible reasons for disparities in graduation rates by race and ethnicity, including differences in family background, differences in ability, discrimination, credit constraints, policies that potentially reduce these disparities (e.g., providing more need-based financial aid), improving preschools or the K–12 education system, and affirmative action in college admissions (Hinrichs, 2014).

Cheng, Suwanakul, and Wu (2015) used institutional data from College Results Online to test the effects of college quality, college cost and financial aid, student characteristics, and local labor market on the completion rates of HBCUs. They found that college quality and college costs were the most important factors influencing graduation rates of HBCUs and, along with financial aid, student characteristics, and local labor market conditions, accounted for 73 percent of the variation in graduation rates among HBCUs. Because college quality has a positive effect, college costs have a negative effect, and financial aid has a positive effect on HBCU graduation rates, improving the quality and reducing the net price of college education can help to improve the graduation rates of minority-serving institutions.

ACTUAL GRADUATION RATES VERSUS PREDICTED GRADUATION RATES

A focus on improving raw graduation rates generally works against MSIs and HBCUs, as it emboldens some institutions to raise admissions standards in order to improve retention and graduation rates and discourages institutions from enrolling and working toward success with students of color who rely on higher education for social and economic mobility.

Alexander Astin, founder of the Higher Education Research Institute (HERI), has long recommended a method of evaluating graduation rates that would take into account the characteristics of students who enroll in different types of colleges, measuring institutional effectiveness by calculating the difference between how many students are expected to graduate and how many actually graduate (DeAngelo et al., 2011). MSIs are likely to enroll students who have lower probabilities for completion, including minority students, low-income students, first-generation students, and academically underprepared students. DeAngelo and colleagues (2011) elaborate:

> Although graduation rates for African Americans are low, African American students are graduating at rates higher than predicted, with differences more pronounced at HBCUs [see figure 5.1]. After four years we predict that only 14.9% of African Americans at HBCUs and 17.3% of African Americans at other institutions would graduate. The actual graduation rate for HBCUs is 20.2% and for other institutions 21.7%. Thus, African American students at HBCUs graduate at a rate 36% higher than predicted as compared with 25% higher than expected at other institutions. After five and six years differences between predicted and actual are much closer at both HBCUs and other types of institutions, but HBCUs continue at each of these marks to do better than expected. Taken together these results again reinforce what has been learned in this study; that much of the difference between institutions in their degree completion rates is attributable to differences in the characteristics and profiles of the enrolled students. (p. 30)

LOW-INCOME STUDENT ENROLLMENT AT MSIs AND HBCUs

A 2006 National Center for Education Statistics (NCES) study surmised that black students were most prevalent in baccalaureate institutions with large low-income enrollments, where they made up 50 percent of freshmen in very selective institutions and 35 percent in minimally selective institutions; many of the 105 HBCUs were included in these two groups of institutions. NCES data show that graduation rates dropped systematically as the size of the low-income freshman population increased, even within the same Carnegie classification and selectivity level (Horn, 2006). One-fifth of NCES's identified low-income serving institutions were HBCUs and were more likely to be minimally selective, to be public or private with religious affiliations, to enroll larger proportions of minority students, and to have smaller undergraduate full-time enrollment.

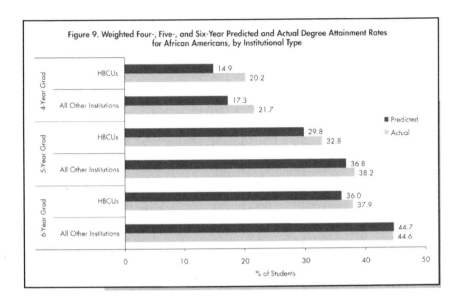

Figure 5.1. *Source:* DeAngelo et al. (2011).

A 2012 United Negro College Fund (UNCF) report found that SAT scores and Pell Grant eligibility, when used as proxies in a multiple-regression model for academic preparedness and socioeconomic status, respectively (alongside an institution's status as an HBCU or non-HBCU), accounted for about half of a student's likelihood of enrolling for a second term and almost two-thirds of the likelihood of graduating. In fact, when regression analysis was used to control for SAT scores and Pell Grant funding, in every case, the inferior performance of HBCUs to non-HBCUs not only was reduced or removed but also was reversed (Richards & Awokoya, 2012). While the majority of HBCUs enroll students with lower SAT scores, more-selective HBCUs that accept only students who are highly prepared for college have higher graduation rates than their less-selective counterparts (Gasman, 2013).

ACCESS AND SUCCESS:
ATTENDING MSIs AND HBCUs

A 2013 study of students enrolling at MSIs in Texas found that the effect of attending an MSI did not have a consistent negative or positive effect on college-graduation outcomes, despite general expectations that MSIs are more likely to underperform in terms of student outcomes than non-MSIs.

Actually, while the demographic characteristics relating to disadvantage remain true in the Texas context, once matched on observable characteristics and controlled for institutional characteristics, it did not appear that attending an MSI hindered graduation outcomes in the Texas postsecondary market for black students who attended an HBCU or for Hispanic students who attended an HSI (Flores & Park, 2015).

In North Carolina, more than half (56 percent) of the black matriculants at the University of North Carolina's (UNC) 16-campus system attend one of the 5 HBCUs (Clotfelter, Ladd & Vigdor, 2015). Findings of the 2015 study by Clotfelter, Ladd, and Vigdor reveal that UNC's HBCUs enroll students who would otherwise most likely not have attended a four-year college, at least not immediately after high school, if those HBCUs did not exist.

MSIs and HBCUs offer many minority students admission often denied to them by the nation's most-selective institutions. The results of a 2014 study suggest that graduation rates of Hispanics and possibly blacks rise when affirmative action is banned at selective colleges, but this may be due to the changing composition of students at these colleges. However, the results of affirmative-action bans on the stock of graduates from selective colleges are more apparent. Because fewer underrepresented minorities are admitted to selective colleges, fewer become graduates of selective colleges (Hinrichs, 2014).

ARE HBCUs OVERPERFORMING?

UNCF study findings in 2012 demonstrate that "HBCUs are high-performing, if often undervalued, assets in serving students and the nation by enrolling, retaining and graduating students whom the country needs to remain economically healthy and internationally competitive" (Richards & Awokoya, 2012, p. 5). In figure 5.2, Richards and Awokoya compare actual HBCU and non-HBCU success rates to estimated success rates.

Actual non-HBCU retention rates were 9 percent higher than they were for HBCUs; however, when SAT scores and Pell Grant funding were controlled for, retention rates for HBCUs would have been 5 percent higher than they were for non-HBCUs. The UNCF study suggests that, if HBCUs and non-HBCUs were to enroll students from the same socioeconomic status and with the same level of academic preparedness, then HBCUs would graduate black students at a higher rate, by 14 percent, than non-HBCUs.

A comprehensive study by Muraskin and Lee (2004) of 20 four-year institutions with large shares of low-income students, 10 with higher-than-average graduation rates and 10 with lower-than-average graduation rates, provides some evidence to suggest that African American students who attend HBCUs have somewhat-higher graduation rates than comparable stu-

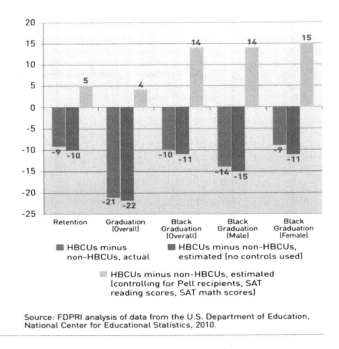

Source: FDPRI analysis of data from the U.S. Department of Education,
National Center for Educational Statistics, 2010.

**Figure 5.2.   Retention and graduation-rate percentage differences, actual and
estimated, 2009. Richards & Awokoya (2012).**

dents who select other schools. Specialized support programs at HBCUs,
such as six-week summer bridge programs, mentoring programs, and black
male initiative programs, contribute to graduation rates that are higher than
expected.

Black male initiatives at HBCUs are credited for increasing black males'
retention and persistence, as well as contributing to their noncognitive development immeasurable by tests and consisting of attitudes, behaviors, and
strategies that are important to the success of black students at HBCUs
(Palmer, Wood, & Arroyo, 2015). For black females attending HBCUs, one
study's results show that family income, hours attempted in year 1 in college,
and hours earned in year 1 in college were predictors of retention, and high
school GPA, college GPA year 1, and college GPA year 4 were predictors of
graduation (Farmer, Hilton, & Reneau, 2016).

One example of HBCU overperformance is the 2011 study "The Relative
Returns to Graduating from a Historically Black College/University," which
found that the treatment effect of graduating from an HBCU relative to a
non-HBCU is positive with respect to labor market and psychological outcomes across three decades. The study results suggest that as HBCUs afford

graduates relatively superior long-run returns they continue to have a compelling educational justification, as the labor market outcomes of their graduates are superior to what they would have been had they graduated from a non-HBCU (Price, Spriggs, & Swinton, 2011). These results support the idea that HBCUs have a comparative advantage in nurturing the self-image, self-esteem, and identity of its graduates, which theoretically matters for labor-market outcomes.

GEORGIA STATE UNIVERSITY:
A CASE STUDY OF MSI OVERPERFORMANCE

Perhaps no better example of overperformance exists in postsecondary education than Georgia State University. Georgia State University is an urban, public, minority-serving institution located in Atlanta. In 2005, the six-year graduation rates for white, African American, and Hispanic students were 32 percent, 26 percent, and 22 percent, respectively. Georgia State's student population of underrepresented minorities increased by 10 percent, from 53 percent in 2008 to 63 percent in 2014, and the percentage of undergraduate Pell Grant recipients increased from 31 percent in 2007 to 59 percent in 2014.

Amid changing demographics, Georgia State was hit with more than $40 million in state budget cuts. Yet, today, without changing their admission criteria and in light of shifting demographics and budgetary restraints, Georgia State is the number one producer of African American baccalaureate degrees in the United States, conferring more than 2,000 degrees to African American undergraduates annually.

In 2015, the six-year graduation rates for white, African American, and Hispanic students had increased to 50.4 percent, 58.4 percent, and 57.6 percent, respectively. Not only did Georgia State increase its graduation rate by more than 20 percent over the course of a decade, but also they completely reversed the minority achievement gap. The National Student Clearinghouse data in 2015 for all four-year college graduates who began at Georgia State as first-time freshmen, the graduation rates for white, African American, and Hispanic students go up to 76.4 percent, 77.5 percent, and 76.7 percent, respectively. A public, urban university that graduates minority, low-income, remedial, and first-generation students at rates of more than 50 percent is an overperformance of about double the expected graduation rate.

Unfortunately, the rules of the college completion game grossly underacknowledge the outstanding accomplishments of a Georgia State University. While Georgia State has gained national recognition for its innovation and unparalleled advances in higher education from Time *magazine, the* New

York Times, *Complete College America, the* Wall Street Journal, *the* Economist, *the Aspen Institute, and even the White House, it has failed to climb the
college rankings lists as should be expected. The college completion game
continues to reward highly selective, exclusive institutions with large endowments and high profiles, leaving many higher-education advocates asking,
"Is the game rigged?"*

THE FUTURE FOR MSIs, HBCUs,
AND COLLEGE COMPLETION

As MSIs, HBCUs, and postsecondary institutions in general are under increasing pressure to graduate more well-prepared students in less time and
for less money, federal and state officials are demanding that those who enter
their public institutions, especially minority, low-income, and underrepresented students, earn a degree. With more than two dozen states disbursing
some state funding based on how many students an institution graduates
rather than how many it enrolls, retaining students is becoming more crucial
to the university bottom line (Ekowo & Palmer, 2017). High expectations
and heightened scrutiny may serve to undermine MSIs and HBCUs with
regard to the future of performance-based funding. A 2014 Southern Education Foundation report highlights several concerns for performance funding
and MSIs:

> Performance Funding policies are challenged by limitations of available data,
> difficulty identifying appropriate metrics for such a diverse set of organiza-
> tions, and the challenges with defining and measuring educational value and
> success. Therefore, many state policy makers should move cautiously in
> adopting these funding models and carefully consider the nation's most vul-
> nerable institutions that are often serving the most neglected student popula-
> tions, public MSIs. (Jones, 2014, p. 3)

Jones outlines five key considerations for developing performance-based
funding for minority-serving institutions: (1) include MSI leaders and experts
in policy development; (2) reconsider the utility of commonly used metrics,
such as graduation and job-placement rates; (3) create metrics that are re-
sponsive to input factors of individual institutions, such as the admission of
low-income, first-generation, and academically underprepared students; (4)
address data capacity before implementing policy to ensure that all campuses
have equitable opportunities to obtain performance funding; and (5) use performance-funding policies to address racial and ethnic equity.

In order for MSIs and HBCUs to win the college completion game, the
so-called rules of the game need to be adjusted to consider more than just raw
graduation rates using the limited NCES/IPEDS calculation by first-time,

freshman cohort each fall. Using expected or predicted graduation rates for student cohorts to better evaluate institutional effectiveness is one important strategy for MSIs and HBCUs. MSIs and HBCUs must be valued as essential partners for the college completion agenda in the United States. Harmon (2012) declares, "MSIs are already contributors to the national college completion goals and should be considered experts in the education of low-income, first generation, and under-represented students."

THE BOTTOM LINE

The nation's MSIs and HBCUs enroll greater percentages of black and Hispanic students than any other institution type. In spite of postsecondary-degree-attainment gaps by race and ethnicity, MSIs and HBCUs often over-perform when predicted graduation rates are calculated using regression analysis to control for household income, first-generation status, and standardized test scores. Ultimately, with national demographics shifting toward a majority minority population, it will be impossible to reach national college completion goals without MSIs and HBCUs producing more graduates of color.

REFERENCES

Cheng, X., Suwanakul, S., & Wu, R. (2015). Determinants of graduation rates of historically black colleges and universities. *Journal of Economics and Economic Education Research*, *16*(2), 51.

Clotfelter, C. T., Ladd, H. F., & Vigdor, J. L. (2015, September). *Public universities, equal opportunity, and the legacy of Jim Crow: Evidence from North Carolina* (NBER Working Paper No. 21577). Cambridge, MA: National Bureau of Economic Research.

DeAngelo, L., Franke, R., Hurtado, S., Pryor, J. H., & Tran, S. (2011). *Completing college: Assessing graduation rates at four-year institutions*. Los Angeles: Higher Education Research Institute, UCLA. Retrieved from https://heri.ucla.edu/DARCU/CompletingCollege2011.pdf.

Ekowo, M., & Palmer, I. (2017, March). *Predictive analytics in higher education: Five guiding practices for ethical use* (Policy paper). Washington, DC: New America, Education Policy.

Farmer, E., Hilton, A. A., & Reneau, F. H. (2016). Variables that contribute to retention and graduation of black American females at an historically black university. *Negro Educational Review*, *67*(1–4), 133.

Flores, S. M., & Park, T. J. (2015). The effect of enrolling in a minority-serving institution for black and Hispanic students in Texas. *Research in Higher Education*, *56*(3), 247–276.

Gasman, M. (2013). *The changing face of historically black colleges and universities*. Philadelphia, PA: Center for Minority Serving Institutions, University of Pennsylvania. Retrieved from https://www.gse.upenn.edu/pdf/cmsi/Changing_Face_HBCUs.pdf.

Harmon, N. (2012, January). The role of minority-serving institutions in national college completion goals. *Institute for Higher Education Policy*. Retrieved from http://www.ihep.org/sites/default/files/uploads/docs/pubs/the_role_of_msis_final_january_20121.pdf.

Hinrichs, P. (2014). Affirmative action bans and college graduation rates. *Economics of Education Review*, *42*, 43–52.

Horn, L. (2006, October). *Placing college graduation rates in context: How 4-year college graduation rates vary with selectivity and the size of low-income enrollment* (NCES 2007-161). Washington, DC: US Department of Education, National Center for Education Statistics. Retrieved from https://nces.ed.gov/pubs2007/2007161.pdf.

Jones, T. (2014, June). *Performance funding at MSIs: Considerations and possible measures for public minority-serving institutions.* Atlanta, GA: Southern Education Foundation. Retrieved from http://www.southerneducation.org/getattachment/38ac1248-3b91-4871-bb8e-f5f28b659b54/Performance-Funding-at-MSIs.aspx.

Muraskin, L., & Lee, J. (2004). *Raising the graduation rates of low-income college students.* Washington, DC: Pell Institute for the Study of Opportunity in Higher Education. Retrieved from https://files.eric.ed.gov/fulltext/ED490856.pdf.

Palmer, R. T., Wood, J. L., & Arroyo, A. (2015). Toward a model of retention and persistence for black men at historically black colleges and universities (HBCUs). *Spectrum: A Journal on Black Men, 4*(1), 5–20.

Price, G. N., Spriggs, W., & Swinton, O. H. (2011). The relative returns to graduating from a historically black college/university: Propensity score matching estimates from the national survey of black Americans. *Review of Black Political Economy, 38*(2), 103–130.

Provasnik, S., & Shafer, L. L. (2004, September). *Historically black colleges and universities, 1976 to 2001* (NCES 2004–062). Washington, DC: US Department of Education, National Center for Education Statistics, Government Printing Office. Retrieved from https://nces.ed.gov/pubs2004/2004062.pdf.

Richards, D. A. R., & Awokoya, J. T. (2012). *Understanding HBCU retention and completion.* Fairfax, VA: Frederick D. Patterson Research Institute, UNCF. Retrieved from http://9b83e3ef165f4724a2ca-84b95a0dfce3f3b3606804544b049bc7.r27.cf5.rackcdn.com/production/PDFs/Understanding_HBCU_Retention_and_Completion.pdf.

Chapter Six

Case Studies

Stories of College Attrition and Student Success

Chapter 4 fully details the many short-term and long-term benefits of earning a college degree. But what about the nearly 50 percent of students, the so-called dropouts, who do not graduate in six years or less at their postsecondary institutions of origin? Are there any benefits of attending college for them? Do they still value college education? Results from a 2009 survey of a nationally representative sample of 614 22- to 30-year-olds with at least some postsecondary education concludes that "it would be a mistake of the highest order to write off young people because they dropped out of college" (Johnson & Rochkind, 2009).

The survey responses suggested that most young adults understand the value of knowledge and grasp the economic benefits of attaining a college degree as well as how life changing a college education can be. According to the survey, the majority of survey respondents wanted to complete college and wished to return to school, but perhaps the most poignant evidence of how the 22- to 30-year-olds felt about college was that even though they themselves left before finishing their degree, and likely will never return to higher education, 97 percent of young American parents who dropped out of college said that they would encourage their own children go to college (Johnson & Rochkind, 2009).

This chapter introduces a number of case studies of successful leaders in the fields of business and entertainment who never completed their college degrees but who support higher education with their time and resources. Many of these leaders, entrepreneurs, and trailblazers often credit postsecondary education for setting them on a path to success. College "drop-outs" Bill Gates, Sean "P. Diddy" Combs, and Mark Zuckerberg are just a few examples of how motivated, inspired, and prepared for lifelong success students can be after several semesters of college matriculation. In fact, the Bill & Melinda Gates Foundation offers the most lucrative and supportive scholarship program in higher education, the Gates Millennium Scholarship.

CASE STUDY: BILL GATES

In a 2016 interview with *Bloomberg*, Bill Gates said that he liked lots of things about college, including the smart people around, being fed, and earning grades that made you feel smart (Weinberger, 2016). He also stated that, despite dropping out of Harvard University in 1975 after less than three years of matriculation, he loved being a student and takes online college courses regularly. In the same interview, he stated that the value of a college degree is easy to underestimate. Consequently, his Bill & Melinda Gates Foundation, perhaps the world's richest philanthropic organization, established college education in the United States as one of its top priorities (Young, 2012).

In 1975, Bill Gates founded Microsoft with his childhood friend Paul Allen. As Microsoft's chief software architect and chairman, Gates led the company to become the worldwide leader in business and personal software, services, and solutions. Under Gates's 40 years of innovative leadership, millions of people have accessed Microsoft software and enjoyed the benefits of personal computing. Almost all Americans, businessmen and -women, chefs, artists, analysts, journalists, nurses, gamers, and more, use Microsoft products on a daily basis (TED, 2018). Gates cocreated the 8080 BASIC computer language in eight weeks on the campus of Harvard University in 1975, which became the de facto standard in the young microcomputer industry. Gates said later, "It was the coolest program I ever wrote" (Wallace & Erickson, 1992, p. 49).

Gates left his full-time position at Microsoft in 2008 to focus on philanthropy as cochair of the Bill & Melinda Gates Foundation. He believes that all lives have equal value; as such, the foundation has donated billions to support HIV and AIDS programs, libraries, agriculture research, disaster relief, global health, and education. It awards grants to reformers at postsecondary institutions who work to fix inefficiencies in higher education that keep many students from graduating on time or at all. It also promotes radical reform in college teaching, advocates a move toward flipped classrooms, spreads best practices in higher education, and views the US education system as a gem that has provided broad opportunity to its citizens and made the country do very well (Young, 2012). In Gates's own words,

> There's nothing that was more important to me in terms of the kind of opportunity I had personally. I went to a great high school. I went to a great university.
> I only went three years, but it doesn't matter; it was still extremely valuable to

me to be in that environment. And I had fantastic professors throughout that whole thing. And so, if every kid could have that kind of education, we'd achieve a lot of goals both at the individual and country level. (Young, 2012, p. 6)

The Gates Millennium Scholars (GMS) program was established in 1999 with a $1.6 billion initiative funded by the Bill & Melinda Gates Foundation with a

goal to promote academic excellence and to provide an opportunity for outstanding minority students with significant financial need to reach their highest potential by:

- Reducing financial barriers for African American, American Indian/Alaska Native, Asian Pacific Islander American and Hispanic American students with high academic and leadership promise who have significant financial need.
- Increasing the representation of these target groups in the disciplines of computer science, education, engineering, library science, mathematics, public health and the sciences, where these groups are severely underrepresented.
- Developing a diversified cadre of future leaders for America by facilitating successful completion of bachelor's, master's and doctoral degrees.
- Providing seamless support from undergraduate through doctoral programs for students selected as Gates Millennium Scholars entering target disciplines.

The benefits of the GMS program are:

- Support for the cost of education by covering unmet need and self-help aid.
- Renewable awards for Gates Millennium Scholars maintaining satisfactory academic progress.
- Graduate school funding for continuing Gates Millennium Scholars in the areas of computer science, education, engineering, library science, mathematics, public health or science.
- Leadership development programs with distinctive personal, academic and professional growth opportunities.

An independent study of the impact of the GMS program by the University of Michigan's Center for the Study of Higher and Postsecondary Education revealed that the program attracts talent from among the most underrepresented students in higher education: low-income and racial and ethnic minorities. According to the study, the method of the program selection and the promise of long-term financial support for each student have the effect of extending opportunity, allowing students to focus on college goals and ultimately ensuring success against the odds typical for the majority of college-bound low-income students (Hurtado, Laird, & Perorazio, 2003).

CASE STUDY: SEAN "P. DIDDY" COMBS

In May 2014, Sean "P. Diddy" Combs (also known as Puff Daddy) delivered the commencement address at Howard University in Washington, DC, and was awarded an honorary doctoral degree in the humanities. Even though he did not complete his undergraduate degree when he matriculated at Howard University, during his commencement address he stated, "Howard University didn't just change my life—it entered my soul, my heart, my being and my spirit" (Peters, 2014).

Combs began his career as an entrepreneur at Howard University, when he arrived as a freshman in 1988. He worked as a party promoter; his weekly hip-hop dance parties were the hottest ticket on Howard's campus. The young business administration major also ran a shuttle service for Howard students to travel to and from the airport and sold T-shirts and sodas on campus. His businesses were so successful while he was a young college student that the Howard University administration contracted his services to assist with the planning of official homecoming events, including the 1989 Howard University homecoming at the Masonic Temple. The university was expecting 1,500 people, but 4,500 attended, forcing DC Metro Police to close off streets for the event (Jones, 2014).

After two years of matriculation, Combs left Howard University to become an intern at Uptown Records in New York City. He was promoted to vice president in less than one year. In 1993, Combs launched his own record label, Bad Boy Entertainment, and worked with such artists as Mariah Carey, New Edition, Method Man, Babyface, TLC, Boyz II Men, Lil' Kim, SWV, Aretha Franklin, Mary J. Blige, Faith Evans, and Biggie Smalls (Biography.com Editors, 2017). After appearances in several movies and television programs, perhaps the pinnacle of Combs's acting career was playing Walter Lee Younger in Broadway's revival of *A Raisin in the Sun*, as well as in the TV adaptation in 2008, for which he received the NAACP Award for Outstanding Actor.

With an estimated net worth of $825 million, Combs has established himself as a rapper, actor, producer, hip-hop mogul, businessman, and entrepreneur of the highest order. As the chairman and CEO of Combs Enterprises, he has a diverse portfolio of businesses and investments covering the music, fashion, fragrance, beverage, marketing, film, television, and media industries, with such companies as Bad Boy Worldwide Entertainment Group, Sean John, Combs Wine & Spirits, AQUAhydrate, Blue Flame Agency, REVOLT Films, and REVOLT Media & TV (Combs Enterprises, 2018).

His philanthropic work and political activism encompass his pledge of 1 million bottles of water and a long-term commitment to provide water to the citizens of Flint, Michigan; the $2 million he raised for New York City public schools and children suffering from HIV and AIDS; and his 2008 voter registration project Vote or Die. In 2016, Combs opened the Capital Prep Harlem, a free public charter school in the Harlem neighborhood of New York City. The school serves grades 6 to 12, with a year-round, college-preparatory education that aims to develop lifelong learners, leaders, and agents of social change (Victor, 2016).

In 2016, Combs surprised Howard University's president from the stage of Verizon Center during his Bad Boy Family Reunion Tour by presenting a $1 million check to the School of Business for scholarships for undergraduate business majors and internships with his companies. In a statement announcing the scholarship, Combs said, "I was blessed to receive a great education from Howard University—one of the best schools in the world—and it helped to fuel my success in business and life. . . . [T]his scholarship will make it possible for the next generation of leaders to pursue their dreams and achieve greatness" (Svrluga, 2016). Recipients of the scholarship participate in summer internships at Bad Boy Entertainment or REVOLT Media & TV, with Combs Enterprises representatives assigned as their mentors.

From Howard University to hip-hop mogul at the top of the *Forbes* list of billionaires, college "dropout" Sean Combs's success cannot be ignored and discounted by traditional postsecondary student success standards.

CASE STUDY: MARK ZUCKERBERG

In February 2004, at age 19, Mark Zuckerberg launched "The Facebook" from his dormitory room at Harvard University. Originally created as an online photo directory to promote social networking for Harvard students, Zuckerberg and his college roommates expanded "The Facebook" to include Stanford, Dartmouth, Columbia, New York University, Cornell, Brown, and Yale and then onto other schools that had social contacts with Harvard (Zuckerberg, 2016). Now, at age 34, Mark Zuckerberg has an estimated net worth of more than $70 billion. In 2017, Facebook had 2.2 billion monthly active users who had logged into the social media platform during the previous 30 days. If Facebook were a country, it would be the third-largest in the world behind China and India (Grossman, 2010).

Zuckerberg supports postsecondary education as a pathway to success. In 2014, he and his wife, Priscilla, a 2007 Harvard graduate, pledged $120 million for education in underserved and low-income San Francisco Bay area communities, including $7.5 million to TheDream.US, a scholarship fund for hundreds of students in the bay area whose parents brought them into the country illegally as children to attend college (Noguchi, 2015). The Zuckerbergs announced the Chan Zuckerberg Initiative in 2015, a philanthropic organization focused on "personalized learning, curing disease, connecting people, and building strong communities." Through the organization, they have pledged $12.1 million to help low-income undergraduate students at Harvard and will provide financial support for up to 2,300 college students to pursue public-service jobs over the next 15 years (Associated Press, 2017). In a 2015 Facebook post, Zuckerberg stated that "we ought to help everyone in our society achieve their full potential."

In 2015, Zuckerberg announced his plans to sell 99 percent of his Facebook shares during his lifetime; he is a member of the Giving Pledge, joining Bill Gates, Warren Buffett, and more than 100 other billionaires vowing to donate the majority of their wealth to philanthropy (Cha, 2015). Zuckerberg said in September 2017 that he planned to sell 35 to 75 million shares over the next 18 months, totaling between $6 billion and $12 billion (Callahan, 2017). According to his Facebook page, some shares will support the Chan Zuckerberg Initiative.

In 2017, 12 years after leaving Harvard to work on Facebook full time, Mark Zuckerberg returned to receive his degree and deliver the university's commencement address, during which he proclaimed,

> My best memory from Harvard was meeting Priscilla. . . . Priscilla and I started dating. And, you know, that movie made it seem like Facemash was so important to creating Facebook. It wasn't. But without Facemash I wouldn't have met Priscilla, and she's the most important person in my life, so you could say it was the most important thing I built in my time here. We've all started lifelong friendships here, and some of us even families. That's why I'm so grateful to this place. Thanks, Harvard. Today I want to talk about purpose. But I'm not here to give you the standard commencement about finding your purpose. We're millennials. We'll try to do that instinctively. Instead, I'm here to tell you finding your purpose isn't enough. The challenge for our generation is creating a world where everyone has a sense of purpose. (Zuckerberg, 2017)

During Zuckerberg's April 2018 testimony in front of the Senate Judiciary Committee and Commerce Committee, he reminisced fondly about his time at Harvard (Annear, 2018).

CASE STUDY: KEVIN LILES

Kevin Liles left Morgan State University (MSU) just 17 credits short of earning an undergraduate degree in electrical engineering. He lost his NASA scholarship just months before his scheduled graduation because of declining grades, as he tried balancing his studies with his full-time job as a supervisor at a travel agency and as a member of his band, Numarx (Liles, 2005). He found himself at a crossroads having to choose between taking out loans to pay for the balance of his degree or pursuing a career as an up-and-coming music producer and manager. Now, as a record executive and entrepreneur, Liles has a net worth of $60 million.

Liles joined Def Jam as an intern in 1991 after he left MSU, rose to president in 1998, and built the label into a global powerhouse with stars like Jay Z, DMX, and Ja Rule (Rys, 2017). In 2004, Liles went to Warner Music Group, where he served as executive vice president until 2009. He left Warner to form KWL Enterprises, which includes a management company that oversees the careers of musicians, athletes, and models, including D'Angelo, Trey Songz, Estelle, Nelly, Selita Ebanks, and many others. In addition to leading KWL Enterprises, Liles founded 300 Entertainment, an entertainment-based content company backed by the likes of Google Ventures.

Liles returned to MSU's campus in 2011 to host the closing awards ceremony of the inaugural Make It Happen Summer Business Institute, a program that hosted Baltimore City and Baltimore County high school juniors and seniors and engaged them in a two-week business-plan competition judged by panel of local entrepreneurs, legislators, and civic leaders (Morgan State University, 2011). His Make It Happen Foundation funded the program, enabling MSU professors, MBA alumni, and undergraduate students to provide instruction on marketing, software, and finance to help the students develop their business plans. In May 2016, MSU awarded the honorary doctor of laws degree to Liles for committing his professional life to enabling others to live out their dreams and for devoting his personal life to philanthropy and community activism that promotes empowerment and education among the youth of Baltimore and beyond.

He returned to MSU's campus again in November 2016 to serve as the keynote speaker for the university's annual Founder's Day Convocation. The occasion was marked by the announcement of the Anniversary Campaign for Morgan State University, chaired by Liles. According to Morgan's president, the campaign is the largest, most ambitious comprehensive campaign in the university's history, as well as of any public historically black college or university (HBCU) in the country (Morgan State University, 2016a). The goal of the Anniversary Campaign is to raise $250 million from private and public sources. "The impact of this comprehensive campaign will be transformative for the students at Morgan, the research being advanced here and the impact this university makes on Baltimore and beyond," said Liles.

He continued, "Morgan State has already made history with a legacy of 150 extraordinary years as a leader in higher education in this country. We are now on track to make history again with this comprehensive campaign, and I am so proud to be a part of it" (Morgan State University, 2016a).

During a 2016 *Forbes* interview, Liles stated, "Most of us did not get to where we are without trials and tribulations. I went to school for electrical engineering and became the CEO of Def Jam. Our paths are written in pencil on purpose. . . . Because of my engineering background, and because of my leadership as a quarterback, all those elements have helped me to freestyle my way to success" (Payne, 2016). Once a noncompleter of college, Dr. Liles continues to give back to MSU, the institution that, in his own words, is a "very special place for me . . . like a safety harness that dropped from above helping me to ease the burden[s], I didn't have to worry about what was behind me, I was able to focus on my future and what was in front of me" (Liles, 2005).

CASE STUDY: CALVIN TYLER

MSU announced its largest individual gift, $5 million, in 2016, from Calvin E. Tyler Jr., a retired UPS senior executive, and his wife, Tina, making it the fifth-largest donation from an individual to any HBCU (Morgan State University, 2016b). Although Tyler entered MSU as a freshman majoring in business administration in 1961, he had to interrupt his matriculation in 1963 because he lacked the funds to continue his enrollment. The newlywed Tyler was faced with providing for his family with a part-time job that didn't pay enough to cover his tuition and household bills (Douglas-Gabriel, 2016). In 1964, he accepted a job as one of the first 10 drivers at UPS in Baltimore. After two years with UPS, he became a manager. Over the course of his 30-plus-year career with UPS, Tyler ascended to serve on the company's board of directors and become senior vice president of operations for UPS, the position from which he retired in 1998 (Morgan State University, 2016b).

Morgan State University's Calvin and Tina Tyler Endowed Scholarship Fund provides need-based scholarships to cover the full tuition for students who reside in the Tylers' hometown of Baltimore City. A native of Baltimore, Tyler was the first person in his family to attend college. Even though he did not finish college, he never forgot how MSU shaped his life. "I learned the value of hard work and I appreciate the education that I got," he said. "I would have preferred to have stayed and finished, but I learned a lot" (Douglas-Gabriel, 2016). Since 2002, the fund has provided full scholarships for more than 200 MSU students, many of whom also are first-generation college students. In Tyler's own words,

> I think anyone who has had any success in life and has the ability to reach back and help others; this is the time for them to do it. There are two major things I want to achieve (with the endowed scholarship fund): Number one, to see as many of our young people graduate with a degree as possible. . . . The second thing that my wife and I are concerned about, and that's why we're providing 10 full-tuition scholarships each year, is that we want more students to get a college degree and graduate debt-free. (Morgan State University, 2016b)

In honor of Tyler and his wife, MSU broke ground for the construction of the new Calvin and Tina Tyler Hall, an $88 million, state-of-the-art facility scheduled to open in 2020. Tyler's personal story of financial struggle while he attended MSU in the 1960s resonates with students. "Every person can do something, and supporting the Tyler scholars is our something," he said. "When we read the letters of appreciation from the scholarship recipients, and when we come here in May and watch our scholars walk across that stage with their degrees, there is no better feeling in the world" (Morgan State University, 2017).

Marybeth Gasman wrote in her 2016 HuffPost blog,

> As I've been researching alumni giving at Historically Black Colleges and Universities (HBCUs) for decades, Tyler's story is particularly interesting to me. To date, I have interviewed over 1,000 alumni about their giving habits and Tyler is different. What we know is that those who don't finish college rarely give back to an institution. We also know that alumni giving rates at HBCUs are low—with those at public HBCUs hovering near 5–6% and those at private HBCUs near 9–10%. Morgan State is doing something different and it's paying off.

Perhaps the difference Gasman speaks of is that, instead of discounting or throwing away students who never finish college, postsecondary institutions can entreat them, partner with them, and connect them to the institution.

MORGAN STATE UNIVERSITY'S "ALMOST ALUMS"

Over the course of my 19 years of employment at MSU, I have observed many students enter and leave the university. Obviously, the desired outcome is an exit from the university via commencement. The unfortunate reality is that many MSU students, just about 60 percent of them in the graduation cohort, do not finish on time in less than six consecutive years. This one statistic is very misleading when it comes to the perception of students' talent and potential.

Three young men come to my mind when I think of our "almost alums" at MSU: Virgo, Ricky, and Randall. All three of these young men exhibited intelligence, charisma, and leadership during their tenure at the university. Each one of them left the university without a degree in hand.

Virgo was an honors student on a full scholarship matriculating into his junior year, when he had an epiphany about the earth and the lifestyle he was leading. He decided to give up the modern luxuries he had been accustomed to and live a simple life, fully sustained by his own hands and natural resources on a secluded farm in another state. He relocated and pursued his dream of an organic and wholesome lifestyle apart from the modern world.

Ricky, who was raised in a two-parent, middle-class home of college graduates, decided to pursue his career in the rap industry after completing only several semesters of matriculation at MSU. Unlike several of the case studies outlined in this chapter, he failed to ever find success in the hip-hop industry. When I last inquired about his progress, a friend of his said that he had gotten a "regular job" and had moved out of his parents' home.

Randall, another university honors scholar, came into his own on the social scene while attending MSU. Once a shy freshman, he quickly blossomed into one of the most popular students on campus. He slipped away from campus at the end of his second year unceremoniously to pursue his social life full time. I've seen his parents in social circles and inquired about his progress; they informed me that he is still quite popular on the social scene and that they long for him to finish his degree.

The reasons for these three young men's departure from postsecondary education are not traditional in the sense that they struggled financially or academically, but rather they took three separate paths in pursuit of other lifestyles. I've learned from my inquiries of them over the years that there is a desire in each one of them that they would one day earn their degrees from Morgan. I wonder how the university could best reengage these young men, all likely in their 30s, and reintroduce them to the college culture. The possibilities are twofold: (1) providing them with a feasible and flexible path to graduation as mature and nontraditional students, and (2) inviting them to be reengaged with the university that first exposed them to the ideas that led to their pursuit of different lifestyles. As it stands now, they're just "dropouts" on paper, a statistic that traditionally represents failure and separation from postsecondary success.

EXCEPTIONS OR THE "NORM"

While it's true that there are successful college dropouts, as this chapter outlines, statistically speaking, these case studies are not the norm. A 2017 study published in the *Conversation* found that the vast majority of the success stories in the United States are college graduates. As Bill Gates has remarked, "Today what they [employers] believe in by and large are degrees. And if you have a great degree then you're considered for jobs, and if you don't have that degree there's a lot of jobs you won't get consideration for" (Young, 2012, p. 3). Because dropping out of college deprives most people of the skills, knowledge, and resources they need to build a good life for themselves, even with a great business idea, it is still recommended that students complete their education first and start their business later (DeMers, 2018).

The value added from even one year of college can be transformative. Each of the case studies in this chapter demonstrate how an intellectual and supportive campus environment that connects students to mentors and like-minded peers can facilitate innovation, entrepreneurship, and leadership that otherwise may have gone unrealized. Although colleges and universities often are indicted when students don't complete college, presently there isn't a national system routinely collecting data about the success of students who attended college but never completed it. The value of any postsecondary education, however, is affirmed to a certain degree by the successful college dropouts highlighted in this chapter who advocate for college completion and continue to support postsecondary education, notwithstanding their own failure to complete an undergraduate degree.

THE BOTTOM LINE

Even though college dropouts often are written off by the higher-education community and society at large, these noncompleters still obtained some benefits from college matriculation. The most compelling evidence of the value of at least some college matriculation is that the overwhelming majority of dropouts, 97 percent, plan to strongly encourage their children to attend college, thus interrupting first-generation college status (Johnson & Rochkind, 2009).

Bill Gates, P. Diddy, Mark Zuckerberg, Kevin Liles, and Calvin Tyler Jr. share several commonalties: (1) They left college before graduating, (2) they value their time spent in college, (3) they continue to support and promote postsecondary education, (4) they invest in higher education by providing college scholarships, and (5) they engage with the institutions they attended. Instead of dismissing college dropouts, postsecondary institutions should consider engaging with noncompleters, not only for the purpose of reclaiming or reenrolling them, but also to engross them in the campus community as partners and advocates.

REFERENCES

Annear, S. (2018, April 11). Mark Zuckerberg couldn't stop mentioning his Harvard dorm room during Facebook testimony. *Boston Globe.*

Associated Press. (2017, November 13). Mark Zuckerberg gives $12M public service grant to Harvard. *Boston Globe.* Retrieved from https://www.boston.com/news/local-news/2017/11/13/mark-zuckerberg-gives-12m-public-service-grant-to-harvard.

Biography.com Editors. (2017, December 19). Sean "P Diddy" Combs biography. *Biography.com.* Retrieved from https://www.biography.com/people/sean-puffy-combs-9542180.

Callahan, D. (2017, September 25). Windfall: As Mark Zuckerberg sells his Facebook stock, get ready for bigger philanthropy. *Inside Philanthropy.* Retrieved from https://www.insidephilanthropy.com/home/2017/9/23/here-comes-the-cash-as-mark-zuckerberg-sells-his-facebook-stock-get-ready-for-bigger-philanthropy.

Cha, A. E. (2015, December 2). With $45 billion pledge, Mark Zuckerberg imagines 'a world without suffering from disease.' *Washington Post.*

Combs Enterprises. (2018). Retrieved from http://www.combsenterprises.com.

DeMers, J. (2018). Are college-dropout billionaire entrepreneurs really that common? *Entrepreneur.* Retrieved from https://www.entrepreneur.com/article/311472.

Douglas-Gabriel, D. (2016, February 10). He couldn't afford to stay at Morgan State, but once he made it he gave back millions. *Washington Post.*

Edwards, H. S. (2015). Why Mark Zuckerberg wants to spend on personalized learning. *Time.* Retrieved from http://www.time.com/4132619/mark-zuckerberg-personalized-learning/.

Foley, E. (2015). Mark Zuckerberg and Priscilla Chan donate $5 million for scholarships for Dreamers. *Huffington Post.* Retrieved from https://www.huffingtonpost.com/2015/06/17/mark-zuckerberg-dreamers_n_7605656.html.

Gasman, M. (2016, February 17). A lesson in donor cultivation: Morgan State University. *HuffPost.* Retrieved from https://www.huffingtonpost.com/marybeth-gasman/a-lesson-in-donor-cultiva_b_9240618.html.

Grossman, L. (2010, December 15). Mark Zuckerberg. *Time.*

Hurtado, S., Laird, T. F. N., & Perorazio, T. E. (2003). The transition to college for low-income students: The impact of the Gates Millennium Scholars Program. *University of Michigan, Center for the Study of Higher and Postsecondary Education.* Retrieved from https://docs.gatesfoundation.org/documents/final-transitiontocollege-hurtado.pdf.

Johnson, J., & Rochkind, J. (2009). *With their whole lives ahead of them: Myths and realities about why so many students fail to finish college* (Public Agenda report). Seattle: Bill & Melinda Gates Foundation.

Jones, J. (2014). *Sean "Diddy" Combs: A biography of a music mogul.* Berkeley Heights, NJ: Enslow.

Liles, K. (2005). *Make it happen: The hip-hop generation guide to success.* New York: Simon and Schuster.

Morgan State University. (2011, August 5). Entertainment exec Kevin Liles returns to MSU for summer business institute ceremony. Retrieved from https://news.morgan.edu/entertainment-exec-kevin-liles-returns-to-msu-for-summer-business-institute-ceremony/.

Morgan State University. (2016a). Morgan State launches $250-million Anniversary Campaign: Entertainment industry giant Kevin Liles lends his support to effort. Retrieved from https://news.morgan.edu/morgan-state-launches-250-million-anniversary-campaign/.

Morgan State University. (2016b). Morgan State receives $5-million scholarship donation: MSU alumnus and wife expand their endowed fund for students from Baltimore City. Retrieved from https://news.morgan.edu/morgan-state-receives-5-million-scholarship-donation/.

Morgan State University. (2017). Morgan State University Breaks Ground on Its New Student Services Building. Retrieved from http://news.morgan.edu/morgan-state-university-breaks-ground-on-its-new-student-services-building/.

Noguchi, S. (2015, June 17). Zuckerberg, Chan fund $5 million for 'dreamer' scholarships. *Mercury News.*

Payne, O. (2016, December 16). Kevin Liles talks #Freestyle50Challenge and gives advice to up-and-coming rappers. *Forbes.*

Peters, M. (2014, May 10). Sean Combs receives honorary degree from Howard University. *Billboard.* Retrieved from https://www.billboard.com/articles/columns/the-juice/6084727/sean-diddy-combs-receives-honorary-degree-from-howard-university-revolt.

Rys, D. (2017, April 6). Kevin Liles talks the past, present and future of 300 Entertainment: Exclusive. *Billboard.* Retrieved from https://www.billboard.com/articles/business/7751460/kevin-liles-300-entertainment-interview-lyor-cohen.

Svrluga, S. (2016, September 23). Sean 'Diddy' Combs gives $1 million to alma mater Howard U.: 'I was blessed.' *Washington Post.*

TED. (2018). Bill Gates: Philanthropist. Retrieved from https://www.ted.com/speakers/bill_gates.

Victor, D. (2016, March 28). Sean Combs to open charter school in Harlem. *New York Times.*

Wallace, J., & Erickson, J. (1992). *Hard drive: Bill Gates and the making of the Microsoft empire*. Chichester, NJ: Wiley.

Weinberger, M. (2016). Bill Gates says he doesn't regret dropping out of Harvard. *Business Insider*. Retrieved from http://www.businessinsider.com/bill-gates-on-dropping-out-of-harvard-2016-10/.

Young, J. R. (2012, June 25). A conversation with Bill Gates about the future of higher education. *Chronicle of Higher Education*.

Zuckerberg, M. (2016). *Mark Zuckerberg*. AV2 by Weigl. Retrieved from https://www.immagic.com/eLibrary/ARCHIVES/GENERAL/WIKIPEDI/W110601Z.pdf/.

Zuckerberg, M. (2017). Mark Zuckerberg's commencement address at Harvard. *Harvard Gazette*. Retrieved from https://news.harvard.edu/gazette/story/2017/05/mark-zuckerbergs-speech-as-written-for-harvards-class-of-2017/.

Chapter Seven

College Attrition and the Popular Culture

This chapter investigates how the media via news, politicians, and entertainment, and popular culture intersect with college attrition and often devalue college education, perhaps serving as a driver of attrition. For more than 40 years, to the most critical skeptics, college has been viewed as "at best a social center or aging vat, and at worst a young folks' home or even a prison that keeps them out of the mainstream economic life for a few more years" (Bird, 1975). Many argue that our current culture places far too much emphasis on attending and graduating from a four-year college after completing an academic program of study in high school, even though only 30 percent of young adults successfully complete this highly touted pathway to success (Symonds, Schwartz, & Ferguson, 2011).

One writer has gone as far as to assert that the value of a college degree has become something of a self-fulfilling prophecy; it's become worth so much because people assume its value is high (Indiviglio, 2010). Indiviglio points out that college graduates often end up in careers that have little or nothing to do with their education, but their college degrees still give them an edge over someone with just a high school diploma because "employers would rather you have studied something irrelevant to the job in college than nothing at all." The *Atlantic* writer admits that saying college is valuable for many young adults is an indisputable claim; however, it may not be valuable for all, or even most, young adults.

ARGUMENTS AGAINST COLLEGE

A Huffington Post blogger maintains that, as a result of technology, higher education in its traditional college setting can never be effective or progressive enough to keep up with the growing needs of employers, who look to college institutions for their future employees; the writer cautions that "anyone who makes the terrible mistake of pursuing a college education in this day and age will live to regret it" (Price, 2014). He continues by offering seven reasons students should not go to college: (1) preparation for the real world, (2) job opportunities, (3) student loans, (4) job readiness, (5) a degree that is obsolete before graduation, (6) conversion to corporate clone, and (7) wasting time. Also, this HuffPost blogger recommends four options students should consider instead of attending college: (1) educate yourself, (2) build a business, (3) build a brand, and (4) go to a vocational or trade school.

One author asks the poignant question, "Should marginally motivated students with mediocre achievement skills go into debt to the tune of $120,000 for tuition loans and the cost of leaving the workforce for 4 to 5 years?" (Hicks, 2015). While the author concedes that college offers many benefits that can't be measured by financial costs, he to the contrary asserts that, unless students have high academic ability, self-control, motivation, and the ability to concentrate, college can be a frustrating and disappointing choice. Since the 2007 recession, many of the most commonly reported stories in the media are about college graduates who live in their parents' basements or who have taken out staggering levels of debt and are unable to repay their loans; they are not college graduates who have obtained jobs and made a good start in life (Hartle, 2017).

One observer of college trends contends that the simple truth is that not all students are eager for continued academic work that seems to be divorced from real-world work. She states that there should be alternatives for those students who seek practical and worthy career choices beyond spending four more years pursuing academic studies and borrowing lots of money for a higher education (Cuban, quoted in Strauss, 2012). Self-made millionaires James Altucher and Grant Cardone strongly recommend alternatives to college, such as obtaining skills online, going to the library and reading books, or simply entering the workforce (Elkins, 2017).

Ironically, Altucher followed a traditional route and matriculated at Cornell University for undergraduate school and attended Carnegie Mellon for graduate school. Although Cardone advocates strongly against college education, he has stated that he will support his children attending an elite postsecondary institution because he acknowledges the value of the networking and relationships built in college.

A 2008 *Wall Street Journal* commentary, "For Most People, College Is a Waste of Time," promotes a CPA-like certification exam system for any college major for which the bachelor's degree is used as a job qualification, such as criminal justice; social work; public administration; and the many separate majors under the headings of business, computer science, and education. The basis of this anticollege argument is that, while a bachelor's degree represents a certain amount of intellectual ability and perseverance, a system of certifications would provide evidence of competence (Murray, 2008).

A shift in guidance counseling advanced the "college for all" paradigm that began in the 1960s, when high school counselors viewed themselves as gatekeepers for postsecondary education, to the 1990s, when counselors recommended college to 66 percent of high school seniors (Clayton, 1999). According to a 2018 *Wall Street Journal* article, a course correction is now rippling through US high schools, as many educators begin to once again emphasize vocational education, rebranded as career and technical education. The Association for Career and Technical Education reported last year that 49 states have enacted 241 policies to support career and technical training (Belkin, 2018).

THE POLITICS OF POSTSECONDARY EDUCATION

Popular radio host and media personality Rush Limbaugh offers bold opinions regarding college education, often badmouthing postsecondary institutions. During a 2018 radio broadcast, Limbaugh expressed the following sentiments:

> Look at what our betters have done to the whole idea of a college education. They've made it unaffordable. What is the value in graduating from four years with debt that could run anywhere from $20,000 to 150,000, and the more you're in school, the higher the debt? And the more debt that a graduate has, the less the value of the degree, the number of years it's gonna take to repay the loans. And in this way, a college education has been warped. And they're in charge of all of it. They're in charge of the tuition. They're in charge of the loan programs. They've taken it over. The government runs all of this. And with grant money involved the government has a say-so in curricula. Look at all of the worthless degrees now that graduates have because they thought it was what they were interested in or meaningful, but it's not. And so they're unemployable, and they have all of this debt. (Limbaugh, 2018)

In recent years, higher education has become a political football and object of derision, especially for some Republican politicians, who prove their conservative bona fides by beating up on colleges (Rampell, 2017).

The Pew Research Center published a study in 2017, "Sharp Partisan Divisions in Views of National Institutions," reporting that the majority of Republicans and Republican-leaning independents (58 percent) now say that colleges and universities have a negative effect on the country, up from 45 percent in 2016. By contrast, the study found that most Democrats and Democratic leaners (72 percent) say that colleges and universities have a positive effect, which is little changed from recent years (Pew Research Center, 2017) (see figure 7.1). Even though partisan divides in the views of some of these institutions have widened in recent years, the Pew study shows that the public's overall evaluations have little changed, with the majority of Americans saying churches and religious organizations (59 percent) and colleges and universities (55 percent) have a positive effect.

DO PARTISAN DIVISIONS DIVIDE?

A 2017 Gallup poll found that 33 percent of Republicans and 56 percent of Democrats were confident in US colleges, a difference of more than 20 percent (Newport & Busteed, 2017). According to the poll, not only were Republicans less confident than Democrats about colleges and universities in general, but also the reasons Republicans gave for these attitudes differ from those provided by the smaller group of Democrats who were negative.

Republicans who maintain low levels of confidence in colleges were most likely to express their belief that colleges and universities are too liberal and

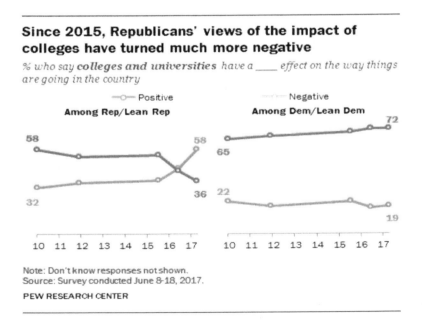

Figure 7.1.

political, that colleges don't allow students to think for themselves and are pushing their own agendas, or that students are not taught the right material or are poorly educated. However, negative Democrats were much more likely to cite issues dealing with practical aspects of higher education, noting that colleges are too expensive or are not well run or have deteriorating quality or that college graduates aren't able to find jobs.

The Gallup finding that US adults are increasingly divided along partisan lines on the issue of higher education may likely have been exacerbated by several high-profile student protests that have spurred debates about free speech and contentious choices for speakers on campus (Newport & Busteed, 2017). Among the top reasons for both Republicans and Democrats expressing high levels of confidence in these institutions are: (1) personal positive experiences with colleges and universities, (2) the belief that colleges are essential for the nation, (3) the belief that colleges are doing a good job of educating students, and (4) the belief that a degree is necessary to get a better job. Gallup researchers ask, To what degree will diminished confidence in higher education among Republicans lead to decreased public support and funding for America's colleges and universities?

A 2017 *Wall Street Journal*/NBC News survey reports that most Republicans, rural residents, and people who consider themselves poor or working class said college isn't worth the cost (Dann, 2017). Those surveyed who were most likely to say that a four-year degree is not worth the cost include rural dwellers (66 percent), white working-class Americans (65 percent), and those with only some college (58 percent) or only a high school education or less (55 percent). Those surveyed most likely to call higher education a good investment include those with a college degree (61 percent) or a postgraduate degree (66 percent), high-income earners (60 percent), and nonwhites (56 percent). The data also found a gender gap in views about the value of a four-year degree, with 53 percent of men saying that a college degree is not worth the cost, while just 41 percent of women said the same.

A senior writer at *Newsweek* reminds us that, when students across the nation protested on the day of Trump's inauguration, they confirmed, "with devastating precision," the conservative critique of higher education (Nazaryan, 2018). In the current partisan environment, public universities have found it even more difficult to navigate the political landscape than private institutions because their fortunes are dependent on elected officials.

The majority of college students in the United States attend a public institution funded in large part by the states, compared to only 16 percent of students who attend a private institution of any kind (Nazaryan, 2018). Despite the Ivy League's outsized place in the popular culture and imagination, the eight Ivy League institutions represent only .04 percent of the nation's collective undergraduate student body.

Another issue confronting higher education is the changing view of truth. Logic, the disinterested search for truth, rigorous scientific research, and empirical verification have been at the heart of higher-education institutions in the modern era; however, for many citizens today, feelings outweigh facts (Hartle, 2017). It has become difficult to convince the public that not all news reports are truthful when the proliferation of information sources has made it easy for people to receive only news and information that confirm their own views.

IS STUDENT LOAN DEBT AN AMERICAN CRISIS?

Recent student loan debt data reported by Student Loan Hero indicate that there is $1.48 trillion in total US student-loan debt, 44.2 million Americans with student-loan debt, a student-loan-delinquency rate of 11.2 percent (90-plus days delinquent or in default), an average monthly student-loan payment of $351 for borrowers aged 20 to 30 years, and a $203 median monthly student-loan payment for borrowers aged 20 to 30 years (Student Loan Hero, 2018).

These data, coupled with an economy weakened by a major recession, have raised serious questions about whether the market for student debt is headed for a crisis, where borrowers unable to repay their loans will have to be bailed out by taxpayers. A Brown Center on Education Policy at Brookings analysis of more than two decades of data on the financial well-being of American households suggests that the reality of student loans may not be as dire as many commentators fear.

The Brookings research team found that roughly one-quarter of the increase in student debt since 1989 can be directly attributed to Americans obtaining more education, especially graduate degrees. While the average debt levels of borrowers with a graduate degree have more than quadrupled, from just under $10,000 to more than $40,000, the debt levels of people who had earned only bachelor's degrees increased by a smaller margin, from $6,000 to $16,000 (Akers & Chingos, 2014). The Brookings data strongly suggest that increases in the average lifetime income of college-educated Americans has more than kept pace with increases in debt loads. In fact, between 1992 and 2010, the average household with student debt saw an increase of about $7,400 in annual income and $18,000 in total debt, where the increase in earnings received over the course of 2.4 years would pay for the increase in debt incurred. The Brown Center on Education Policy at Brookings analysis further states,

> The monthly payment burden faced by student loan borrowers has stayed about the same or even lessened over the past two decades. The median borrower has consistently spent three to four percent of their monthly income on

student loan payments since 1992, and the mean payment-to-income ratio has fallen significantly, from 15 to 7 percent. The average repayment term for student loans increased over this period, allowing borrowers to shoulder increased debt loads without larger monthly payments. These data indicate that typical borrowers are no worse off now than they were a generation ago, and also suggest that the borrowers struggling with high debt loads frequently featured in media coverage may not be part of a new or growing phenomenon. The percentage of borrowers with high payment-to-income ratios has not increased over the last 20 years—if anything, it has declined. (Akers & Chingos, 2014)

One economist asserts that there is no debt crisis because student-debt levels are not large relative to the estimated payoff of a college education in the United States (Dynarski, 2015). Instead, he diagnoses a repayment crisis caused by student loans being paid when borrowers' earnings are lowest and most variable. There is a mismatch in the timing of the arrival of the benefits of college and its costs; ironically, this mismatch is the very motivation for providing student loans in the first place.

Dynarski proposes an income-based repayment structure for student loans, with a longer window for repayment than the 10 years that is currently the standard. Dynarski argues that a well-structured repayment program would insure borrowers against both micro- and macroshocks. His proposal could be self-sustaining, with an interest rate that would appropriately account for the government's borrowing and administrative costs, as well as for default risk.

THE CHOICE NOT TO ATTEND COLLEGE

When people know that someone works at a college or university, that employee of the institution is often put in a position to serve as a liaison, a recruiter, or a spokesperson for not only their college or university but also for postsecondary education in general. Over the course of my nearly 20 years in higher education, I have answered many questions about whether college is worth it. My extended family, my church members, and people whom I know through casual associations have at one time or another asked me to meet with them, their son or their daughter, their sister or their brother, or someone that they know in reference to attending college.

On the positive side, I have led many people through the admissions process, many of whom are now successful professionals working in their chosen fields and have earned graduate degrees and terminal degrees. Unfortunately, on the negative side, I have observed many students make decisions not to matriculate and instead leave behind untapped potential for greatness.

For example, one young lady from my church, after coming to a public historically black college or university (HBCU) for a visit per my coordination, decided to attend a private, predominantly white university instead because popular culture and stereotypes led her to believe that the white university would be better for her. What she and her parents failed to realize was that the white university charged three times the tuition and fees of the HBCU. She was literally locked out of her dorm room after one semester of matriculation, owing a bill of approximately $15,000, which needed to be paid before the university would release her transcript so that she could attend any other postsecondary institution. The last time I saw this bright, young woman, she was working full time at a sandwich shop, still trying to repay her $15,000 debt. She told me that she wished she had attended the HBCU with affordable tuition.

Another young student whose parents asked me to investigate the possibility of their daughter earning a track scholarship at Morgan State University (she had been one of Maryland's top track stars in high school) decided to accept an offer at Temple University after I had arranged a campus visit for her and introduced her to MSU's track coach. Unfortunately, she never enrolled at Temple University because, once she received the total cost of attendance, her family realized that her track scholarship would barely cover one-third of her total costs. The last time I encountered this young lady at the mall, she was a single mother with two children, and she expressed to me that her dream was still to attend college one day.

Two young men whom I mentored after first asking me about college told me that they had decided to just go straight into the workforce after high school in order to earn money. More than five years later, one of these young men is unemployed and is living with his mother, and the other young man has a part-time job working at a private school as a teacher's assistant. I have no doubt that stereotypes about what's wrong with college, the looming burden of student-loan debt, and the positive branding of the elite institutions and private colleges contribute negatively to the decisions that young people make about college, decisions that will forever change the course of their lives.

UNVEILING THE TRUTH ABOUT ATTENDING COLLEGE

One truth about college matriculation is that those high school counselors who steer students away from postsecondary education could be accused of lowering expectations for some students, to the point of educational redlining, because many students who drop out of college are black or nonwhite Hispanics (Steinberg, 2010). Regrettably, perpetuating fallacies and dissuading students from attending college only widen income, race, and gender gaps. A *Time–Money* article, "What's Really Wrong with College Today?" encapsulates the myths and realities about college:

> Pity the poor souls sending their sons and daughters off to college next fall. A chorus of commentators are eager to tell them that tuition in public higher education is "skyrocketing" because profligate college administrators are adding recklessly to their bloated staffs, or that the economy is awash in unemployed college graduates to a point where degrees no longer pay. And even if a lucky graduate nails down a job, some claim, all of her earnings will go to whittling down that mountain of debt that has been piled on her. The good news about college is that none of these hyperbolic statements is true, or even close to it. The bad news is that the atmosphere of crisis bred by these wild assertions distracts us from the very real and quite serious problems besetting American higher education. (Bowen & McPherson, 2016)

Notwithstanding the success of the high-profile college "dropouts" outlined in chapter 6 and the self-made millionaires mentioned in this chapter, the fact remains that the vast majority of leaders in the United States are college graduates. A 2017 study investigated how many of the wealthiest and most influential people graduated from college. The study of 11,745 US leaders, including CEOs, federal judges, politicians, multimillionaires and billionaires, business leaders, and the most globally powerful men and women, found that approximately 94 percent of leaders attended college, and about 50 percent attended an elite school (Wai & Rindermann, 2017) (see figure 7.2).

As income inequality has widened, a terribly uneven playing field has emerged in postsecondary education, where children of affluent parents tend to do well in the current system; they are eight times more likely to earn college degrees than their low-income counterparts (Symonds, Schwartz, & Ferguson, 2011). Meanwhile, middle-class children are often forced to juggle college with work and take out student loans, and low-income children receive little financial assistance or crucial social-network resources, making them far less likely to complete college or enter promising careers. A culture that demonizes college education actually promotes the status quo by relegating many low-income families to limited options with low returns; even some college education has the potential to break through generational barriers.

Some scholars warn against overlooking the intangible benefits of any college experience, regardless of whether a degree is earned. Though students may not apply what they learn in college directly to their chosen work, some college experience contributes to aesthetic appreciation, better health, and better voting behavior (Steinberg, 2010). Particularly in the context of the war on postsecondary education in the media, popular culture, and politics, a college degree still offers the best opportunity for upward mobility in

The myth of the successful dropout

In a study of 11,745 successful individuals from across the U.S., we found that the vast majority of the country's leaders attended college – many of them elite schools.

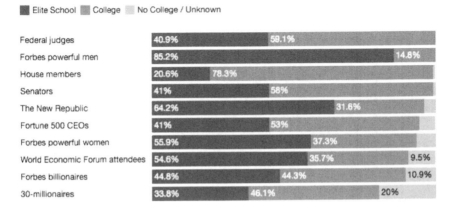

Figure 7.2.   *Source:* **Wai & Rindermann (2017).**

American society. More than four decades ago, one of the most cynical critics of postsecondary education confessed,

> But bad as it is, college is often preferable to a far worse fate. It is better than the drudgery of an uninspiring nine-to-five job, and better than doing nothing when no jobs are available. For some young people, it is a graceful way to get away from home and become independent without losing the financial support of their parents. And sometimes it is the only alternative to an intolerable home situation. (Bird, 1975)

THE BOTTOM LINE

Bloggers, radio hosts, and celebrities at times downplay, discount, and discourage college attendance. Numerous high school guidance counselors carefully select whom they recommend college attendance to; for some it has become less uncommon to recommend vocational education and apprenticeships. To some extent, the topic of college matriculation has become a type of political football, as a number of Republicans view postsecondary institutions as breeding factories for liberal ideology.

Contributing greatly to the growing cultural tone of disparagement toward postsecondary education is the student-loan-debt crisis. The cost of college attendance has been increasing steadily, but this chapter shows that increases in average lifetime earnings of college-educated Americans have kept pace with increasing college costs. The myriad benefits of college attendance are well outlined in chapter 4. Regardless of popular awareness, the value of a college education endures.

REFERENCES

Akers, B., & Chingos, M. M. (2014, June). Is a student loan crisis on the horizon? *Brown Center on Education Policy at Brookings*. Retrieved from https://www.brookings.edu/wp-content/uploads/2016/06/Is-a-Student-Loan-Crisis-on-the-Horizon.pdf.

Belkin, D. (2018, March 5). Why an honors student wants to skip college and go to trade school. *Wall Street Journal*.

Bird, C. (1975). College is a waste of time and money. *Psychology Today, 8*(12), 28–35.

Bowen, W., & McPherson, M. (2016, April 8). What's really wrong with college today? *Money*. Retrieved from http://time.com/money/4284269/whats-really-wrong-with-college-today/.

Clayton, M. (1999, October 19). Is college for everyone? *Christian Science Monitor*. Retrieved from https://www.csmonitor.com/1999/1019/p15s1.html.

Dann, C. (2017, September 7). Americans split on whether 4-year college degree is worth the cost. *NBC News*. Retrieved from https://www.nbcnews.com/politics/first-read/americans-split-whether-4-year-college-degree-worth-cost-n799336

Dynarski, S. M. (2015). An economist's perspective on student loans in the United States. Retrieved from http://www.econstor.eu/bitstream/10419/12319/1/cesifo_wp5579.pdf/.

Elkins, K. (2017, July 11). Self-made millionaires say you should think twice before going to college. *CNBC*. Retrieved from https://www.cnbc.com/2017/07/11/self-made-millionaires-dont-go-to-college.html.

Hartle, T. W. (2017, July 19). Why most Republicans don't like higher education. *Chronicle of Higher Education*. Retrieved from https://www.chronicle.com/article/Why-Most-Republicans-Don-t/240691.

Hicks, M. R. (2015, February 15). Is college a waste of time and money? *Psychology Today*. Retrieved from https://www.psychologytoday.com/us/blog/digital-pandemic/201502/is-college-waste-time-and-money.

Indiviglio, D. (2010, May 17). Should more people skip college? *Atlantic*. Retrieved from https://www.theatlantic.com/business/archive/2010/05/should-more-people-skip-college/56821/.

Limbaugh, R. (2018, March 6). College doesn't make sense for everyone. *Rush Limbaugh Show*. Retrieved from https://www.rushlimbaugh.com/daily/2018/03/06/college-isnt-for-everyone/.

Murray, C. (2008). For most people, college is a waste of time. *Forensic Examiner, 17*(4), 32.

Nazaryan, A. (2018, February 1). What is college good for? Absolutely nothing, say Republicans (and some Democrats). *Newsweek*. Retrieved from https://www.newsweek.com/2018/02/09/what-college-good-796253.html.

Newport, F., & Busteed, B. (2017, August 16). Why are Republicans down on higher ed? *Gallup*. Retrieved from http://news.gallup.com/poll/216278/why-republicans-down-higher.aspx?g_source=POLITICAL_PARTIES&g_medium=topic&g_campaign=tiles.

Pew Research Center. (2017, July 10). Sharp partisan divisions in views of national institutions: Republicans increasingly say colleges have negative impact on U.S. Retrieved from http://www.people-press.org/2017/07/10/sharp-partisan-divisions-in-views-of-national-institutions/.

Price, M. (2014, June 17). 7 reasons why you shouldn't go to college and 4 things to do instead. *HuffPost*. Retrieved from https://www.huffingtonpost.com/michaelprice/7-reasons-why-you-shouldn_1_b_5501111.html.

Rampell, C. (2017, December 28). Why do so many Republicans hate college? *Washington Post*.

Steinberg, J. (2010, May 15). Plan B: Skip college. *New York Times*.

Strauss, V. (2012, December 6). Why everyone shouldn't go to college. *Washington Post.*

Student Loan Hero. (2018, May 1). A look at the shocking student loan debt statistics for 2018. Retrieved from https://studentloanhero.com/student-loan-debt-statistics/.

Symonds, W. C., Schwartz, R., & Ferguson, R. F. (2011). *Pathways to prosperity: Meeting the challenge of preparing young Americans for the 21st century.* Cambridge, MA: Pathways to Prosperity Project, Harvard University Graduate School of Education.

Wai, J., & Rindermann, H. (2017, April 19). The myth of the college dropout. *Conversation.* Retrieved from https://theconversation.com/the-myth-of-the-college-dropout-75760.

Chapter Eight

Half-Full and Half-Empty

The Completers versus the Noncompleters

Chapter 9 examines what postsecondary institutions are doing to graduate more students, but this chapter explains the contributing factors at the student level in terms of why some students graduate and others don't. Specifically, what are the reasons for student attrition, what are the characteristics of students who persist in college versus students who leave college without graduating, and what essential characteristic does a successful college student possess? One scholar's answer is self-knowledge. When students have self-knowledge, they become self-directed, eager, energized, and self-motivated; they automatically set meaningful goals and seek ways to achieve them (Daley, 2010).

The underlying causes that lead to dropouts are complex and include an amalgam of poverty, illiteracy, weak family structure, inadequate parenting, and an overburdened basic education system (Daley, 2010). According to Daley, the typical student has two great problems before arriving at college: (1) many are unprepared for the rigors of college academically, and (2) they don't know why they are in college. These two circumstances collide with a third problem in college that causes a crisis for some students—having so little time to prove themselves in an academic term where they must either pass and persist or leave college.

WHO ARE TODAY'S COLLEGE STUDENTS?

The stereotype of college students in the 20th and 21st centuries has been a profile of 18-year-olds, fresh out of high school; leaving middle-class, two-parent homes; heading off to achieve their clearly envisioned goals; full of ambition; and well-prepared for the rigors of higher education. This stereo-type assumes that students will find a way to pay for college, have a place to live on campus while matriculating in college, and come to college with the social and emotional supports required to succeed in college. Contrary to this profile, 21st-century college students work more than 20 hours per week (45 percent), are less likely to attend a residential college (25 percent), and some have dependent children (23 percent) (Johnson & Rochkind, 2009).

Race and gender gaps characterize postsecondary student populations. For example, women make up 71 percent of all student-parents, and roughly two million students, or 43 percent of the total student-parent population, are single mothers (Gault, Reichlin Cruse, & Román, 2014). An Institute for Women's Policy Research (IWPR) analysis of 2011–2012 data from the US Department of Education, National Center for Education Statistics, found that nearly half of all black women in college had dependent children (47 percent), followed by roughly two in five American Indian or Alaska Native and Native Hawaiian or Pacific Islander women (41 percent and 39 percent, respectively).

Differences by race and ethnicity go beyond the home life of students. For example, black and Hispanic students are more likely to receive their post-secondary credential from for-profit schools; schools that spend less money on their students; and schools with lower average SAT scores, lower faculty salaries, lower retention rates for first-year students, and higher stu-dent–faculty ratios (Libassi, 2018).

Highlights from the *Chronicle of Higher Education*'s 2011 almanac in-clude the following statistics (O'Shaughnessy, 2011):

- The annual family income of more than 47 percent of undergraduates is less than $40,000.
- The annual household income of 4.5 percent of undergrads is at least $160,000.
- Twenty-four percent of all first-time undergraduates take at least one re-medial course.
- Only 0.4 percent of undergraduates attend one of the Ivy League schools.
- Approximately 9 percent of students attend flagship universities and other state institutions that conduct intensive research.
- Seventy-three percent of students attend all types of public colleges and universities.
- Just 16 percent of students attend private nonprofit colleges and univer-sities.

More than half of all undergraduates live at home to make their degrees more affordable, about 25 percent work full time and go to school full time, and a quarter of undergraduates are older than 25 (Mellow, 2017). Mellow states that, while tuition for low-income students may be covered by federal financial aid programs, other costs, such as housing, transportation, food, and child care, regularly pose obstacles to education.

Financial pressures like these can make studying full time very difficult, especially because many students' jobs are part time and pay the minimum wage. Mellow asserts that students' work schedules can vary wildly, stretching students so thin that each day can become an ordeal.

STUDENTS WORKING WHILE MATRICULATING

The Georgetown University Center on Education and the Workforce's analysis of 2012–2013 US Census Bureau's American Community Survey data found that nearly 14 million people, 8 percent of the total labor force and a consistent 70 percent to 80 percent of college students, are both active in the labor market and formally enrolled in some form of postsecondary education or training. The 21st-century young, working learners face barriers that their grandparents did not encounter, including the rising cost of college.

Today's undergraduate students are largely relying on student loans to pay for tuition, books, equipment, and other lifestyle needs, with 45 percent of young, working undergraduates earning 200 percent of the poverty level ($23,540) or less (Carnevale, Smith, Melton, & Price, 2015). *Learning while Earning: The New Normal* (2015) examines the students who combine work with ongoing learning through postsecondary education and outlines these findings:

- Going to college and working while doing so is better than going straight to work after high school because students who complete college degrees while working are more likely over time to transition to managerial positions with higher wages than people who go straight into full-time work after high school.
- Working while attending college hurts disadvantaged students the most; low-income students, especially low-income African Americans and Hispanics, tend to experience the more negative effects of working on their educational achievement and attainment.
- Working and learning simultaneously has benefits, especially when students work in jobs related to what they study.
- Most students are working. From 1989 to 2008, between 70 percent and 80 percent of undergraduates were employed, but in 2012, that share had declined to 62 percent due to the job losses associated with the 2007–2009 recession.
- One-third of working learners are 30 or older.

- More people are working full time while in college; approximately 25 percent of all working learners are simultaneously employed full time and enrolled in college full time.
- Students can't work their way through college anymore. The cost of college now makes that impossible; a student working full time at the federal minimum wage can earn $15,080 annually before taxes, not enough to pay tuition at most colleges, much less room and board and other expenses.
- Students are working and taking out more loans to pay for college; the amount of outstanding student-loan debt has increased from $240 billion in 2003 to $1.2 trillion today.

Students surveyed by Public Agenda supported options that would give them more flexibility in scheduling and help them mitigate the challenge of working and going to school at the same time. Eight in 10 of those who did not complete college supported two proposals that they believe would make college graduation feasible: (1) making part-time students eligible for more financial aid (81 percent said this would help "a lot"), and (2) offering more courses in the evening and on weekends so that they could continue working while taking classes (78 percent said this would help "a lot"; Johnson & Rochkind, 2009).

WHY DON'T STUDENTS GRADUATE?

Just more than half of all undergraduates who enroll at four-year colleges as first-time, full-time freshmen in a fall term graduate in six years or less, so should it be expected that 100 percent of students graduate? Velez (2014) identifies several reasons some level of college noncompletion can be expected: (1) Students make their decision to enter college based on limited information, (2) some students on the margin of college entry may need to experience one year of college to obtain more information, and (3) students may experience unforeseen shocks during college that cause them to exit early. Even when prior achievement, test scores, and various motivational factors are taken into account, one study found that coming from an intact and socially economically advantaged family fosters degree completion (Astin & Oseguera, 2005b).

Rising tuition costs, poor academic preparation and study skills, minimal student support and advisory services in higher education, too many young people going to college even though they really do not want to, and too many college professors and advisers complaining that degree completion is the student's responsibility have been cited as potential reasons for student attrition (Bowen, Chingos, & McPherson, 2009). Additionally, four-year-college dropouts have considerably lower high school achievement than four-year-college completers, suggesting that poor academic preparation may be a leading cause of college dropouts (Velez, 2014). Working while in college, living at home, and experiencing personal and family-related stressful events during the college years significantly decrease the odds of graduating (Wilbur & Roscigno, 2016).

Many factors associated with student retention and attrition have been identified in the literature: students who are ill prepared for higher education; the inverse correlation between the economy and college enrollment, which shows that enrollment tends to rise as a recession worsens; student finances and funding for college; increased numbers of at-risk high school graduates enrolling in college; federal and state legislation aimed at increasing postsecondary enrollment and graduation rates; institutions reforming and restructuring their existing programs; institutions introducing peer collaboration, tutorial groups, and teamwork to create student interaction and engagement; and, institutions providing aggressive academic advising, monitoring student progress, and mentoring programs (Mortagy, Boghikian-Whitby, & Helou, 2018). One study found that living at home during college decreases a student's chances of completing a bachelor's degree by about 35 percent (Wilbur & Roscigno, 2016).

WHAT PREDICTS STUDENT SUCCESS?

Crossing the Finish Line: Completing College at America's Public Universities (Bowen, Chingos, & McPherson, 2009) uses data on the approximately 125,000 members of the 1999 entering cohort at 21 prestigious, research-intensive flagship universities, all members of the Association of American Universities and widely regarded as leaders in American higher education, including four state higher-education systems (Maryland, North Carolina, Ohio, and Virginia). It outlines several takeaways from predictive modeling:

- High school grades are a far better incremental predictor of graduation rates than are SAT and ACT scores.
- Overreliance on SAT and ACT scores in admitting students can have an adverse effect on the diversity of the student bodies enrolled by universities.
- The strong predictive power of high school GPA holds, even when little is known about the quality of the high school attended.
- Scores on achievement tests, especially Advanced Placement tests, are better predictors of graduation rates than are scores on the standard SAT and ACT tests.
- Colleges and universities should use a judicious combination of information, including high school GPA, achievement test results, writing skills

test results, and the quality of the high school, in conjunction with standard SAT and ACT scores.

- High schools should not be encouraged to "teach to the test" when the test measures reasoning skills and general aptitude; instead, more weight should be given to content-based tests that measure how well students learn what high school classes aim to teach.

Even though the predictive power of such traditional criteria as gender, ethnicity, parental outcome, and education vary from study to study, standardized test scores and high school grades have consistently been shown to be among the strongest predictors of degree attainment for undergraduate students. Social integration also has emerged as a correlate associated with degree completion. Astin and Oseguera (2005a) find that self-ratings of academic ability, drive to achieve, and intellectual self-confidence are positively predictive of degree completion. Several national studies have used cooperative institutional research program (CIRP) data to identify that joining a fraternity or sorority, participating in volunteerism or community service, being elected to student office, maintaining a social-activist agenda, and participating in student groups are additional correlates of degree completion for undergraduate students (Astin & Oseguera, 2005b).

Seven findings emerge from *Undergraduate Completion and Persistence at Four-Year Colleges and Universities: Completers, Persisters, Stopouts, and Dropouts*: (1) Degree completion was lower than anticipated from a review of literature, (2) completion was more timely and at a higher rate in independent colleges and universities than at public institutions, (3) black and Hispanic completion rates lagged seriously behind those of whites and Asian Americans, (4) the greatest enrollment loss occurred during the first year and after the eighth semester, (5) both socioeconomic status and academic ability influenced persistence, (6) the cumulative effect of socioeconomic status and ability was greater than the influence of either factor by itself, and (7) students who received grants in their first year of study were more likely to remain enrolled than students without grants (Porter, 1989).

FIRST-GENERATION AND LOW-INCOME STUDENTS

The Condition of Education, which includes a special focus essay (Choy, 2001) on the access, persistence, and success of first-generation students (students whose parents did not attend college) in postsecondary education, surmises,

> Whether high school graduates enroll in postsecondary education and whether postsecondary students reach their degree goals depend on many factors, but those whose parents have no education beyond high school are considerably

less likely to succeed than those whose parents have completed a bachelor's degree. Students who are non-white or from low-income families tend to be disproportionately represented among those whose parents have low education. Multivariate analysis confirms that parents' education remains significant for gaining access to postsecondary education and for persistence and bachelor's degree attainment at 4-year institutions even after controlling for other factors such as income, educational expectations, academic preparation, parental involvement, and peer influence.

First-generation students are nearly 70 percent less likely than their non-first-generation counterparts to enroll in a four-year college and nearly 60 percent less likely to graduate from college than their peers (Wilbur & Roscigno, 2016). Wilbur and Roscigno's findings partly tie these disadvantages to socioeconomic status (SES); however, the first-generation disadvantage persists even when SES is accounted for. Students with low socioeconomic and first-generation status are surely at the greatest disadvantage, but Wilbur and Roscigno find that, even as SES increases, the first-generation disadvantage is not eliminated. Likewise, students whose parents did not go to college receive less assistance from their parents in applying to colleges, and yet they are not more likely to receive help from their schools in applying to colleges (Choy, 2001).

First-generation students are significantly more likely to work for the purpose of paying tuition, fees, and living expenses and likely to work more hours per week. Long work hours arguably make it more difficult for students to integrate into extracurricular activities and other dimensions of college life (Wilbur & Roscigno, 2016). One study observes that minority, low-income, and first-generation college students who drop out of four-year colleges had relatively low predicted probabilities of success, while rural dropouts had relatively high probabilities of success (Velez, 2014). First-generation students, on average, are significantly more likely to experience personal and family-related stressful life events during their college years (Wilbur & Roscigno, 2016). First-generation students are less likely to be involved in extracurricular and high-impact curricular activities, such as research with a faculty member and study-abroad programs. A rigorous high school curriculum helps mitigate the disadvantage of first-generation status (Choy, 2001).

STAYING VERSUS LEAVING: MYTHS VERSUS REALITIES

With Their Whole Lives Ahead of Them (Johnson & Rochkind, 2009), a Public Agenda report prepared with support from the Bill & Melinda Gates Foundation, outlines four myths and realities regarding why so many students leave college without graduating:

- **Myth No. 1:** Most students go to college full time. If they leave without a degree, it's because they're bored with their classes and don't want to work hard.

  Reality No. 1: Most students leave college because they are working to support themselves and going to school at the same time. At some point, the stress of work and study just becomes too difficult.
- **Myth No. 2:** Most college students are supported by their parents and take advantage of a multitude of available loans, scholarships, and savings plans.

  Reality No. 2: Young people who fail to finish college are often going it alone financially. They're essentially putting themselves through school.
- **Myth No. 3:** Most students go through a meticulous process of choosing a college from an array of alternatives.

  Reality No. 3: Among students who don't graduate, the college-selection process is far more limited and often seems happenstance and uninformed.
- **Myth No. 4:** Students who don't graduate understand fully the value of a college degree and the consequences and trade-offs of leaving school without one.

  Reality No. 4: Students who leave college realize that a diploma is an asset, but they may not fully recognize the impact dropping out of school will have on their future.

Working while matriculating and going it alone can certainly make the difference between staying and leaving college once students arrive on campus; however, entering college on solid academic footing also contributes to whether students stay or leave college. Regardless of institution type, students who enter college with an A grade point average are four times more likely to finish college then students with a C grade point average or less (Astin & Oseguera, 2005a). Astin and Oseguera confirm, too, that women are more likely than men to attain bachelor's degrees regardless of the time period or category of institution.

There are choices college students make that influence college completion, as well, such as participation in extracurricular activities, experiential learning, and peer-mentoring programs. Wilbur and Roscigno (2016) find that participation in extracurricular activities while in college increases a student's chances of graduating by nearly half, and participation in multiple high-impact activities can increase the chances of completion by nearly 15 percent. Also, students who get involved in community service, clubs, and groups enjoy a greater likelihood of degree completion, whereas noninvolvement in college, especially as students are distracted by full-time work or missing classes, is negatively related to degree completion (Astin & Oseguera, 2005b). College-specific experiences (i.e., involvement in extracurricular

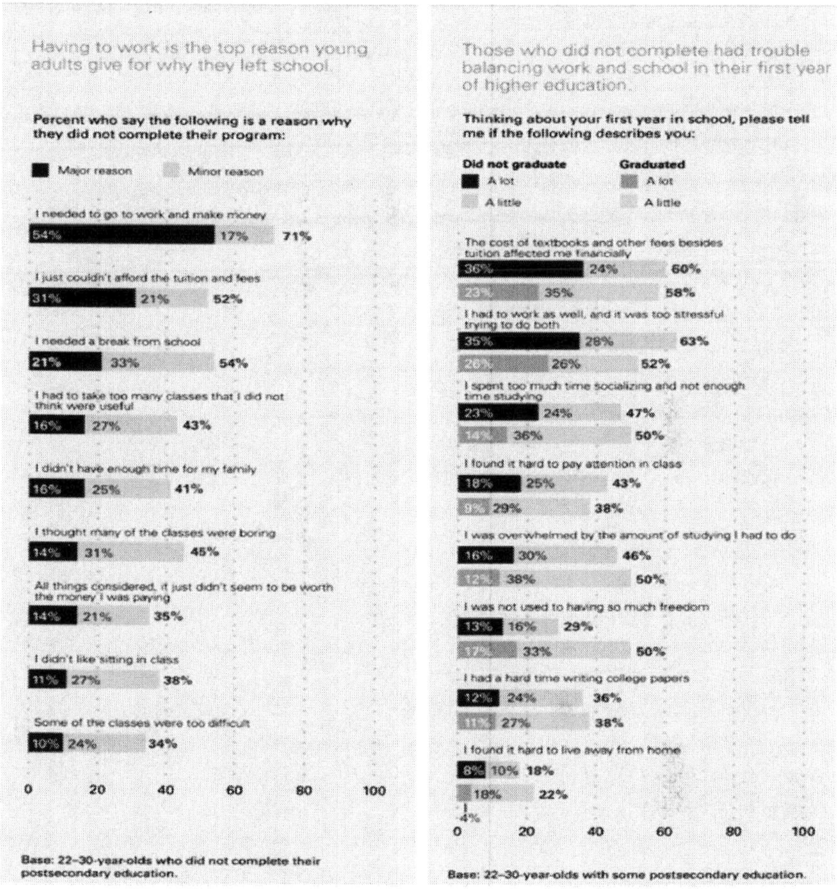

Having to work is the top reason young adults give for why they left school.

Percent who say the following is a reason why they did not complete their program:

■ Major reason   ▨ Minor reason

- I needed to go to work and make money: 54% | 17% | 71%
- I just couldn't afford the tuition and fees: 31% | 21% | 52%
- I needed a break from school: 21% | 33% | 54%
- I had to take too many classes that I did not think were useful: 16% | 27% | 43%
- I didn't have enough time for my family: 16% | 25% | 41%
- I thought many of the classes were boring: 14% | 31% | 45%
- All things considered, it just didn't seem to be worth the money I was paying: 14% | 21% | 35%
- I didn't like sitting in class: 11% | 27% | 38%
- Some of the classes were too difficult: 10% | 24% | 34%

0 20 40 60 80 100

Base: 22–30-year-olds who did not complete their postsecondary education.

Those who did not complete had trouble balancing work and school in their first year of higher education.

Thinking about your first year in school, please tell me if the following describes you:

Did not graduate (■ A lot / ▨ A little)   Graduated (■ A lot / ▨ A little)

- The cost of textbooks and other fees besides tuition affected me financially: 36% | 24% | 60% ; 23% | 35% | 58%
- I had to work as well, and it was too stressful trying to do both: 35% | 28% | 63% ; 26% | 26% | 52%
- I spent too much time socializing and not enough time studying: 23% | 24% | 47% ; 14% | 36% | 50%
- I found it hard to pay attention in class: 18% | 25% | 43% ; 9% | 29% | 38%
- I was overwhelmed by the amount of studying I had to do: 16% | 30% | 46% ; 12% | 38% | 50%
- I was not used to having so much freedom: 13% | 16% | 29% ; 17% | 33% | 50%
- I had a hard time writing college papers: 12% | 24% | 36% ; 11% | 27% | 38%
- I found it hard to live away from home: 8% | 10% | 18% ; 18% | 22% ; 4%

0 20 40 60 80 100

Base: 22–30-year-olds with some postsecondary education.

Figure 8.1. *With Their Whole Lives Ahead of Them*, myth and reality no. 1. *Source:* Johnson & Rochkind (2009).

activities) and particularly high-impact curricular activities (i.e., study abroad, research with a faculty member) strongly increase the likelihood of graduating (Wilbur & Roscigno, 2016).

STUDENTS NEED MONEY AND MOTIVATION

Every academic term at Morgan State University (MSU), students are dropped for nonpayment after late registration ends. Retention rates are always above 80 percent before course schedules are dropped, and then the rates go down into the low 60s after the drop. A proactive reinstatement

process reengages students in the financial-clearance process and reenrolls
students over a period of two weeks, while they continue to attend classes,
resulting in final retention rates in the 70s.

Since 2011, MSU has had a retention rate above 70 percent. What we
have learned is that, when 90 percent of undergraduate students depend on
financial aid and 60 percent are Pell-eligible, low-income students and more
than half of students are first-generation students, students need both money
and motivation to stay in college. Of course, the less unmet financial need a
student has, the more likely they are to graduate. However, beyond just the
financial need, students must have the motivation to push through grueling
financial-aid processes and confusing and often-cumbersome institutional
practices to get financially cleared.

Many students, especially freshmen, are reluctant to raise their hands
and ask for help. They need gentle nudges and clearly mapped-out instruc-
tions in order to navigate the process of financial clearance. Some students
are living on their own without any parental support, while others are first-
generation students whose parents have never participated in financial
clearance at the college level, or students' parents are so busy working
multiple jobs to help support students that it leaves little time for them to
guide students through the process. The motivated students will persevere;
unfortunately, students who lack motivation may more easily succumb to the
financial pressures.

Likewise, working students require motivation to stay engaged in the
classroom while working part-time and full-time jobs to help offset the ex-
penses of their college education. Examples cited in this chapter suggest that
students who participate in activities outside of the classroom are more likely
to finish college, as are students who have parental support. But the stresses
of paying for college and needing to work drive many students to leave
college without graduating. I submit that money and motivation undergird
students completing college more than any other factors.

GRIT?

Grit is defined as a person's trait-level perseverance and passion for long-
term goals, thus influencing their attitudes and behavior across diverse con-
texts (Duckworth, Peterson, Matthews, & Kelly, 2007). Duckworth and colleagues' research over the past decade has focused on noncognitive skills,
skills and traits other than intelligence that contribute to human development
and success. They have developed a test called the "Grit Scale," where students rate themselves on a series of 8 to 12 items. Even though the "Grit
Scale" assessment is entirely self-reported, they have found that a person's

self-reported grit score is highly predictive of achievement under challenging circumstances.

Within the context of postsecondary education, grit is portrayed as a potentially important influence on such outcomes as a student's engagement, achievement level, retention, and probability of graduation (Wolters & Hussain, 2015). The so-called grittier students persevere through adversity and maintain their pursuit of challenging, long-term goals, such as earning a college degree. Wolters and Hussain's research suggests that students' engagement in self-regulated learning may serve as one key pathway through which grit leads to academic success in college. Wolters and Hussain find that, even when accounting for their value and self-efficacy, students who perceived themselves as more diligent and effortful workers also tended to report increased use of cognitive, metacognitive, motivational, and time-management strategies central to self-regulated learning. Likewise, students who report greater consistency in pursuing their established goals also tend to report increased use of time- and study-environment-management strategies.

Three meta-analytic findings from a 2017 study indicate that a crucial reappraisal of the grit construct is warranted; findings reported do hold some promise for proponents of grit as a predictor of success and as a potential focus of interventions (Credé, Tynan, & Harms, 2017). Credé, Tynan, & Harms conclude that grit predicts retention approximately as well as many more traditional predictors of retention, such as cognitive ability and high school grades, although not as well as some other noncognitive predictors, such as perseverance. The study surmises that study skills and study habits, adjustment to college, and class attendance are far more strongly related to academic performance and retention than grit and that there is sound evidence that interventions can improve students' standing on these constructs, especially for study skills and habits.

WHAT CAN STUDENTS DO?

Ultimately, degree completion is a complex phenomenon that can be affected by a variety of student pre-enrollment characteristics, environmental contingencies, and institutional characteristics (Astin & Oseguera, 2005b). Although researchers suggest that such approaches as mentoring programs are helpful in increasing retention, many implementations of these approaches are passive, and students must initiate membership or participation. A more effective approach may be for postsecondary institutions to require participation in student-success programs; moreover, institutions must have annual assessment of all retention initiatives (Mortagy, Boghikian-Whitby, & Helou, 2018). Another study's findings suggest that degree completion can be enhanced if more students are provided with opportunities to live on campus and more opportunities are created for part-time employment on campus (Astin & Oseguera, 2005b).

A 2004 meta-analysis of psychosocial and study skills as predictors of college outcomes distinguishes three types of predictors of college success: (1) such traditional predictors as standardized test scores, high school rank, and GPA; (2) such demographic predictors as socioeconomic status, race, and gender; and (3) such psychosocial predictors as social involvement, motivation, self-management, and study habits (Robbins, Lauver, Le, Davis, Langley, & Carlstrom, 2004).

While students have no control over their socioeconomic status, race, ethnicity, and gender and little control over the rigor of their high school education or their ability to score well on standardized tests, in college they can be encouraged to get involved in extracurricular activities and to become engaged with faculty, advisers, and peers on college campuses in an effort to foster degree completion and academic excellence.

THE BOTTOM LINE

There are many student-level variables associated with college completion or noncompletion; however, there are some characteristics that successful completers have in common, such as working fewer hours, getting involved in cocurricular activities, living on campus, and possessing motivation and self-efficacy. Noncompleters are likely to work more hours, live with their parents, and endure stressful events. Regardless of students' precollege characteristics, such as high school GPA and standardized test scores, there are behaviors that students can adopt to increase the likelihood of completion. Postsecondary institutions should work to encourage students to exhibit behaviors associated with student success and degree completion rather than to succumb to behaviors associated with student attrition.

REFERENCES

Astin, A. W., & Oseguera, L. (2005a, January). *Degree attainment rates at American colleges and universities: Revised edition.* Los Angeles: Higher Education Research Institution, UCLA.

Astin, A. W., & Oseguera, L. (2005b). Pre-college and institutional influences on degree attainment. In A. Seidman (Ed.), *College student retention: Formula for student success* (pp. 245–276). Westport, CT: Praeger.

Bowen, W. G., Chingos, M. M., & McPherson, M. S. (2009). *Crossing the finish line: Completing college at America's public universities.* Princeton, NJ: Princeton University Press.

Carnevale, A. P., Smith, N., Melton, M., & Price, E. (2015). *Learning while earning: The new normal.* Washington, DC: Georgetown University Center on Education and the Workforce.

Choy, S. (2001). *Students whose parents did not go to college: Postsecondary access, persistence, and attainment* (NCES 2001-126). Washington, DC: US Department of Education, National Center for Education Statistics.

Credé, M., Tynan, M. C., & Harms, P. D. (2017). Much ado about grit: A meta-analytic synthesis of the grit literature. *Journal of Personality and Social Psychology, 113*(3), 492.

Daley, F. (2010). Why college students drop out and what we do about it. *College Quarterly, 13*(3).

Duckworth, A. L., Peterson, C., Matthews, M. D., & Kelly, D. R. (2007). Grit: Perseverance and passion for long-term goals. *Journal of Personality and Social Psychology, 92*(6), 1087.

Gault, B., Reichlin Cruse, L., & Román, S. (2014). *College affordability for low-income adults: Improving returns on investment for families and society* (Report# C412). Washington, DC: Institute for Women's Policy Research.

Johnson, J., & Rochkind, J. (2009). *With their whole lives ahead of them: Myths and realities about why so many students fail to finish college* (Public Agenda report). Seattle: Bill & Melinda Gates Foundation.

Libassi, C. J. (2018, May 23). The neglected college race gap: Racial disparities among college completers. *Center for American Progress.* Retrieved from https://www.americanprogress.org/issues/education-postsecondary/reports/2018/05/23/451186/neglected-college-race-gap-racial-disparities-among-college-completers/.

Mellow, G. O. (2017, August 28). The biggest misconception about today's college students. *New York Times.*

Mortagy, Y., Boghikian-Whitby, S., & Helou, I. (2018). An analytical investigation of the characteristics of the dropout students in higher education. *Issues in Informing Science and Information Technology, 15*, 249–278.

O'Shaughnessy, L. (2011, September 6). 20 surprising higher education facts. *U.S. News and World Report.* Retrieved from https://www.usnews.com/education/blogs/the-college-solution/2011/09/06/20-surprising-higher-education-facts.

Porter, O. F. (1989). *Undergraduate completion and persistence at four-year colleges and universities: Completers, persisters, stopouts, and dropouts.* Washington, DC: National Institute of Independent Colleges and Universities.

Robbins, S. B., Lauver, K., Le, H., Davis, D., Langley, R., & Carlstrom, A. (2004). Do psychosocial and study skill factors predict college outcomes? A meta-analysis. *Psychological Bulletin, 130*(2), 261.

Velez, E. D. (2014). America's college drop-out epidemic: Understanding the college drop-out population. *American Institutes for Research.* Retrieved from https://www.air.org/resource/america-s-college-drop-out-epidemic-understanding-college-drop-out-population.

Wilbur, T. G., & Roscigno, V. J. (2016). First-generation disadvantage and college enrollment/completion. *Socius: Sociological Research for a Dynamic World, 2*, 1–11. doi:10.1177/2378023116666.

Wolters, C. A., & Hussain, M. (2015). Investigating grit and its relations with college students' self-regulated learning and academic achievement. *Metacognition and Learning, 10*(3), 293–311.

Chapter Nine

It's Not a Deficit Model

Increasing Retention and Fostering Completion

This chapter outlines best practices for increasing retention and graduation rates from the "value-added" perspective and encourages colleges and universities not to rely on deficit modeling for college completion efforts. It is tempting to dwell on the deficits of students, whether their financial deficits or inability to pay for postsecondary education or academic deficits or lack of college readiness or preparation. More than 50 years of higher-education research has identified effective strategies and best practices to increase retention and foster degree completion at the nation's four-year postsecondary institutions. Pioneers in student retention, student engagement, and student success theory and practice, such as Vincent Tinto, Arthur Chickering, and George D. Kuh, are highlighted in this chapter.

STUDENT RETENTION: HISTORICAL CONTEXT

More than 40 years ago, student retention in higher education and student attrition were typically viewed as a reflection of students' individual attributes, skills, and motivation. Students who did not stay in college were thought to be less able, less motivated, and less willing to defer the benefits that college graduation was believed to bestow; students, instead of institutions, were seen as failing (Tinto, 2006). Tinto asserts that, like any early body of work, preliminary studies of student retention lacked complexity and detail and primarily were drawn from quantitative studies of largely residential universities and students of majority backgrounds.

Tinto thoroughly outlines his theory of student departure from postsecondary education in the 1987 book *Leaving College: Rethinking the Causes and Cures of Student Attrition.* His theory proposes that student attrition is the result of both the social and intellectual college environment and the students' experiences at the college. He suggests that the quality of faculty–student interaction and the student's integration into the college are central factors in student attrition. Tinto further submits that retention lies in a college's commitment to students through the development of effective retention programs with well-timed college actions and establishing appropriate variations in institutional policy necessary for different types of students. Tinto (2004) condenses 25 years of research on student retention and successful retention programs into several institutional actions that enhance retention and graduation:

1. Provide students clear guidelines for what they have to do to be successful; effective advising is an essential part of successful retention programs.
2. Provide academic, social, and personal support; whatever the form, successful retention efforts must empower students to access support when needed.
3. Carefully assess institutional activities, as well as students' activities, and provide frequent feedback.
4. Involve students with other students, faculty, and staff, paying particular attention to those activities that are directed toward student learning; students who are actively involved with peers, faculty, and staff, especially in learning activities, are more likely to learn, persist, and graduate.

Chickering and Gamson (1987) outline seven principles to help improve undergraduate education: (1) Encourage contact between students and faculty, (2) develop reciprocity and cooperation among students, (3) use active-learning techniques, (4) give prompt feedback, (5) emphasize time on task, (6) communicate high expectations, and (7) respect diverse talents and ways of learning. Chickering and Gamson offer the following examples of best practices for postsecondary education: freshman seminars on important topics taught by senior faculty; learning groups of five to seven students who meet regularly during class to solve problems set by the instructor; active learning using structured exercises, discussions, team projects, and peer critiques, as well as internships and independent study; and mastery learning, contract learning, and computer-assisted instruction approaches, which require adequate time on learning.

After these seven principles of good practice were authored in 1987, new communication and information technologies became major resources for teaching and learning in higher education. In 1996, Chickering and Ehrmann recommended cost-effective and appropriate ways to use computers, video, and telecommunications technologies to advance the seven principles. They offer two major conclusions: (1) Institutional policies concerning learning resources and technology support need to give high priority to user-friendly hardware, software, and communication vehicles that help faculty and students use technologies efficiently and effectively, and (2) investments in professional development for faculty members, plus training and computer-lab assistance for students, will be necessary if learning potentials are to be realized.

HIGH-IMPACT PRACTICES IN
POSTSECONDARY EDUCATION

In 2008, Kuh proposed to increase student success in postsecondary education by making it possible for every student to participate in at least two high-impact activities, one in the first year and one taken later in relation to the major field. Kuh lists the following high-impact practices identified in educational research as those that increase rates of student retention and student engagement: first-year seminars and experiences, common intellectual experiences, learning communities, writing-intensive courses, collaborative assignments and projects, undergraduate research, diversity and global learning, service learning and community-based learning, internships, and capstone courses and projects. These practices have been widely tested and shown to be beneficial for college students from many backgrounds; however, on most college campuses, utilization of active-learning practices is unsystematic, to the detriment of student learning (Kuh, 2008).

In 2009, Brownell and Swaner reviewed four high-impact practices: first-year seminars, learning communities, service learning, and undergraduate research. The most common outcome across all four practices was student persistence at a given institution, followed closely by academic performance, usually defined as grade point average. For both of these measures the result was positive: Students who participated in these activities consistently persisted at a higher rate than those who did not. Additionally, all four practices were shown to lead to higher rates of faculty and peer interaction, and three of the four led to increases in critical thinking and writing skills, greater appreciation of diversity and diverse viewpoints, and higher levels of engagement, both in and out of the classroom (Brownell & Swaner, 2009).

A 2015 report used ordinary least-squares-regression analyses to study the effects of participation in the 10 high-impact educational practices endorsed by the Association of American Colleges and Universities (AAC& U) on a variety of liberal arts educational outcomes (Kilgo, Sheets, & Pascarella, 2015). These practices are first-year seminars, academic learning communities, writing-intensive courses, active and collaborative learning, undergraduate research, study abroad, service learning, internships, and capstone courses and experiences. Results suggest that active and collaborative learning as well as undergraduate research had broad-reaching positive effects across multiple liberal arts learning outcomes, such as critical thinking, need for cognition, and intercultural effectiveness. Several other high-impact practices, including study abroad, internship, service learning, and capstone courses and experiences, focused more narrowly on the positive effects on student learning. The most significant practical implication for institutions of higher education is to provide students with opportunities to engage in high-impact practices, particularly such practices as undergraduate research and active and collaborative learning, which are shown to have vast positive impacts for student learning and development (Kilgo, Sheets, & Pascarella, 2015).

MILLENIALS VS. GENERATION Z

In an effort to understand the obstacles and enablers that millennial freshmen faced when transitioning into a college environment, a 2014 qualitative study explored the opinions and perceptions of freshmen and sophomores who had dropped out of college. The study results reveal four core themes that served as either obstacles or enablers for millennial freshmen college students and influenced the transition into the college environment: freshmen-focused activities, effective study skills, instructor–student relationships, and academic advisement-support (Turner & Thompson, 2014).

In order to create a seamless social and academic transition into the college environment, Turner and Thompson (2014) report that millennial freshman students required ongoing academic guidance, a collaborative and interactive learning environment, and skill-development training during the first year. They suggest that institutions could benefit greatly from constructing aggressive academic advisement-support mechanisms or conducting an extensive reevaluation of already-existing programs to create a balanced academic and social experience for new students.

According to the 2016 book *Generation Z Goes to College*, Generation Z students (the students born after millennials) prefer intrapersonal learning on their own so that they are able to learn independently at their own pace. Generation Z students describe themselves as responsible, determined, and thoughtful and prefer to use learning methods that require self-reliance. Technology for the Generation Z student contributes to their preference for working alone, with 85 percent of students reporting engaging in online research or assignments and using technology to access information with little need for interaction with others (Seemiller & Grace, 2016).

While Generation Z students were found to prefer intrapersonal learning on their own, they also enjoy working in groups and desire social learning; therefore, educators can play a large role in the learning experience for Generation Z students. Seemiller and Grace suggest that postsecondary institutions provide engaging and passionate instructors for Generation Z students who do not prefer traditional lectures. Additionally, Generation Z students may benefit from flipped classrooms; hybrid learning; and assignment binging, where, just like television binging, students can complete multiple assignments back to back in one weekend.

With the rising cost of higher education, more than any previous generation, Generation Z students can benefit from access to funding for college. Seemiller and Grace recommend that postsecondary institutions consider centralizing all external scholarships in a database so that students can easily find funding opportunities they are eligible for and apply online for multiple scholarships simultaneously. Additional strategies for retaining Generation Z students include integrating modern learning in the cocurriculum, offering student-selected community-engagement experiences, connecting students' passions to their practices, guaranteeing internship opportunities early on, requiring experiential learning, offering social entrepreneurship courses for nonbusiness majors, and creating opportunities for real-life problem solving (Seemiller & Grace, 2016).

FIRST-GENERATION STUDENTS

Research suggests that colleges and universities consider the entire first-generation student experience from the transition to college and the first year through to graduation when employing enrollment-management resources to increase first-generation students' likelihood of success (Ward, Siegel, & Davenport, 2012). The challenge for campuses is to focus resources so that they reach the particular range of students who are most likely to benefit from engagement opportunities. To counteract the negative effects of first-generation status, Ward, Siegel, and Davenport recommend that colleges and universities specifically target first-generation students for outreach and transition programs, knowing that students are more likely to persist and attain success in college if they feel connected to the institution and feel supported in their curricular and cocurricular endeavors.

Tinto (2004) recommends that colleges and universities do the following to enhance their retention and graduation of first-generation, low-income students:

- Provide financial support in an amount and form that enables low-income students to attend full time rather than part time and, when necessary, work fewer hours, preferably on campus rather than off campus.
- Emphasize academic support and what it takes to be successful in college to address the fact that many low-income students begin college with inadequate academic skills.
- Provide faculty, staff, and peer advising, counseling, and mentoring.

Peer-to-peer programs led by first-generation students who themselves are extending a hand up academically and socially to others who come from similar backgrounds and home situations are gaining traction on campuses nationwide (Tucker, 2014). The abundance of initiatives that US colleges have undertaken to increase the enrollment of first-generation and low-income college students and boost their financial aid include:

- **Norfolk State University's Spartans Preparing for Academic Rigor in College (SPARC):** A four-week summer-bridge program that brings newly admitted freshmen to campus before the school year begins for a few weeks of college immersion and classes to ease the transition from high school to college. Students then become part of the historically black college's Breakfast Club, a yearlong faculty-to-student mentoring program that meets about once a month at 7 a.m. so that students can huddle with their college mentors to get career advice and professional development guidance and hear from special guests.
- **Kenyon College's Kenyon Educational Enrichment Program (KEEP):** A highly selective liberal arts school in Ohio brings students of color to campus over the summer for intensive writing and data-analysis coursework and pairs them with mentors from the faculty or administration. Then they are tracked throughout their college careers, and they receive academic and career-planning advice, as well as access to peer-tutoring/.
- **Chief Dull Knife College:** A tribal community college in Montana uses a combination of faculty engagement, computerized tutoring, and peer feedback to help students conquer mathematics courses.
- **Claflin University's Learning in Communities for Success (LinCs):** In Orangeburg, South Carolina, this school enrolls students in its innovative program designed for first-generation college students and initially funded as part of the Wal-Mart initiative. Freshmen are enrolled together in three team-taught courses: University 101, a freshmen-orientation course that covers the basics of college life, including time management, note taking, and campus resources; English 101, freshmen English composition; and Math 111.

- **Franklin & Marshall College:** Some 70 rising seniors from high schools around the country this past summer participated in a three-week F&M College Prep program. The highly selective, small, liberal arts college in Lancaster, Pennsylvania, gives high school seniors the opportunity to learn together what the college experience is all about. Students in the program spend two hours a day, four days a week, in courses taught by faculty members and complete a research project (Tucker, 2014).

Ward, Siegel, and Davenport propose that a comprehensive approach to student learning and developmental goals that integrates student affairs, enrollment management, and academic affairs units has the best chance of improving support for first-generation students. Because the success and retention of first-generation students is not solely the responsibility of one office or division on campus, it is imperative that a cross-divisional review take place to identify programs and services across the campus to support these goals. Likewise, modeling through predictive data analytics can be a useful strategy in the retention of first-generation students by targeting intrusive services that are proactive, intentional, and prescriptive for first-generation students (Ward, Siegel, & Davenport, 2012).

PREDICTIVE ANALYTICS

Data analytics in higher education encompasses database systems that store large quantities of longitudinal data on students, including very specific transactions and activities on learning and teaching. When students interact with learning, advising, and early-alert technologies, they leave behind data trails that can reveal their sentiments, social connections, intentions, and goals (Daniel, 2015). Researchers can use data analytics to examine patterns of student performance over time, from initial enrollment to degree completion. The added value of data analytics is the ability to turn data into usable information by identifying patterns and deviations from patterns.

Daniel (2015) defines *predictive analytics* as "estimating likelihood of future events by looking into trends and identifying associations about related issues and identifying any risks or opportunities in the future." Therefore, predictive analytics can reveal hidden relationships in data that might not be apparent with descriptive models, such as demographics and completion rates. Predictive analytics can be used to help advisers track students who are exhibiting risk behaviors early in the semester that might result in dropping out or failing a course. Predictive analytics also can help faculty track predicted course-completion rates and design customized content in a course directly correlated to student success.

Borray (2017) recognizes that the most common use of predictive analytics in higher education is in the area of academic success, where course-enrollment patterns and grades, as well as other demographic information, is used to predict a student's risk score, enabling institutions to focus efforts and resources to support their student-success strategies. A 2017 *New America* policy paper, *Predictive Analytics in Higher Education: Five Guiding Practices for Ethical Use* (Ekowo & Palmer, 2017), outlines five guiding principles to consider as administrators formulate how to use predictive analytics ethically:

Guiding Practice 1: Have a vision and plan.
Guiding Practice 2: Build a supportive infrastructure.
Guiding Practice 3: Work to ensure proper use of data.
Guiding Practice 4: Design predictive analytics models and algorithms that avoid bias.
Guiding Practice 5: Meet institutional goals and improve student outcomes by intervening with care.

Analyzing past student data to predict what current and prospective students might do has helped many institutions meet their annual enrollment and revenue goals with more targeted recruiting and more strategic use of institutional aid (Ekowo & Palmer, 2017). While predictive analytics has afforded colleges the opportunity to better customize their advising services and personalize learning in order to improve student outcomes, it is crucial for institutions to use predictive analytics ethically.

Georgia State University (GSU), a pioneer in the realm of predictive analytics, recently added financial analytics to its professional advising model. An early-warning system, similar to its early-alert system for academic concerns, uses predictive analytics to identify red flags in students' finances, such as making late payments on bills, past-due balances, unsubmitted FAFSAs, failure to send required verification documents to receive financial aid, and unmet need (McNeal, 2016). GSU advisers proactively reach out to students in an effort to resolve students' financial issues. Since 2012, Georgia State University has used predictive analytics to mine more than 10 years of student academic data, such as course enrollments and grades, to identify risk factors associated with students failing a course or leaving the university. GSU's academic alerts have resulted in more than 50,000 one-on-one meetings between students and academic advisers per year.

RECLAIMING STOP-OUTS AND NEAR-COMPLETERS

In response to attainment goals and workforce needs, states are aiming to reach near-completers through legislation and initiatives, working to bring them back into a postsecondary institution to complete a credential (Anderson, 2017). As states seek to reengage the near-completer student population, Anderson suggests the following:

- A strong marketing outreach campaign to include postcards, flyers, e-mails, television or radio spots, and individualized URLs proves to be vital in reengaging near-completers.
- States might consider reviewing existing legislation to align new initiatives with current policy, such as reverse-transfer policies.
- Because affordability tends to be an issue for adult learners, states might consider specific postsecondary financing opportunities that cater to the adult learner and their possible need to attend part time, online, or in a competency-based education (CBE) environment.
- States should evaluate the current data available and assess how to use it for student identification and outreach.
- States and institutions should consider flexibility in course scheduling, availability of online learning, ability to earn college credits through prior learning assessments, and CBE models.
- Because many adult learners need social supports, aligning education-funding policies with social-support policies, including housing, food, and child care, can help adult students access these resources.

In 2013, the state of Maryland established a program to help institutions identify, contact, reenroll, and graduate near-completers as one strategy in a larger set of the state's policy efforts aimed to achieve increased college attainment. In Maryland, estimates showing that 66 percent of jobs in 2020 would require a postsecondary credential helped to drive efforts to quickly bring near-completers to completion (Shulock & Moore, 2014).

Administered by the Maryland Higher Education Commission (MHEC), Maryland's One Step Away (OSA) program provides competitive grants to public and private nonprofit two- and four-year colleges to identify, contact, reenroll, and graduate near-completers. Students who have earned a significant number of required credits for an associate or bachelor's degree but who are no longer enrolled in college are targeted. To meet the state's completion goals, the MHEC estimates that the state's postsecondary institutions would need to increase degree production by 2.25 percent annually, for a total of 55,000 degrees to be awarded by 2025, 10,500 degrees above the current annual number (Shulock & Moore, 2014). Policies and practices were adjusted in an effort to adapt to the changing student population, with growing numbers of nontraditional students now representing a majority of enrollment in the state's colleges and universities.

In 2011, Morgan State University independently piloted its own completion initiative that targets students who failed to reenroll but are in good academic standing and with at least 90 credits and encourages them to reenroll (Shulock & Moore, 2014). Morgan's Reclamation Initiative informed the final design of the OSA grant program. MHEC learned of Morgan State's efforts through its submission of a required annual report and has since awarded two OSA grants to the university to support the continuation of its efforts.

Maryland's OSA pilot year of implementation resulted in eight institutions receiving an average of $56,000 through the program; institutions successfully contacted 1,684 former students who met the program requirements. Shulock and Moore (2014) report that, of those successful contacts, 17 percent (292 individuals) reenrolled, and within a 9-month period, 10 percent of the 292 reenrolled students earned a degree. Some of the reclaimed students received a degree almost immediately due to resolved administrative issues, such as missing paperwork or unpaid fines.

RETAINING MINORITY STUDENTS

A 2016 analysis of 232 four-year institutions over a period of 10 years shows that graduation rates for black students at these institutions improved 4.4 percent, compared with 5.6 percent for white students (Nichols, Eberle-Sudré, & Welch, 2016). With graduation rates for black students showing less progress, a widening gap between the completion rates of white and black students exists. Closing the degree-attainment gap for minority students requires increases in graduation rates for minority students at a much faster pace. At Ohio State University, graduation rates for black students have increased by 25.6 percent, and the gap in graduation rates between black and white students has narrowed by 8.6 percent (Zatynski, 2016).

Ohio State's success in retaining minority students is the result of a three-pronged approach to boosting retention and completion among black students on campus beginning in middle school. First-generation, low-income, black middle-schoolers in nine cities across Ohio are connected to college early on; then, for college they receive need-based scholarships for four years, enroll in a three-week summer-bridge program, meet monthly with a success coach, and connect weekly with an upperclassman peer mentor. The supports for these students continue throughout their matriculation, resulting in increased graduation rates for black students and a narrowing gap between black and white students (Zatynski, 2016). Ohio State endeavors to serve as a hub for research, discussion, and sharing of best practices that attract, retain, and encourage college completion among black students nationwide. Similar to Ohio State, postsecondary institutions are challenged to consider equity and attainment in the context of their mission and vision:

> If schools are to take academic equity seriously, they need to recognize first that judgments about who is likely to succeed in a given field are inevitably affected by implicit bias and structural racism and may be wrong about many students of color. Second, to the extent that students of color disproportionately receive lower K–12 academic preparation, institutions should reorient their practices to recognize that education is about more than cream skimming; to truly be an excellent academic institution, a college needs to be able effectively serve any student who meets its admission criteria. Many institutions have been leaders in providing resources to at-risk students through programs like summer bridge, which allow students to adjust to college life before school begins, and through extensive tutoring and academic support programs. (Libassi, 2018)

Over the years, remediation and developmental education in higher education have become contentious issues. Research suggests that, when it comes to retaining minority students, the issue of developmental education cannot be overlooked. If postsecondary institutions were to adopt a policy of not admitting students who need remedial or developmental course work into four-year institutions, then minority students would be negatively affected. Despite the fact that minority students are more likely to take remedial and developmental courses, 50 percent of African American bachelor-program graduates and 34 percent of Hispanic bachelor-program graduates successfully graduate after taking remedial course work (Attewell, Lavin, Domina, & Levey, 2006). If these students were denied entry to postsecondary institutions, then a large portion of minority students would not receive degrees.

The results of a 2010 study suggest that increases in student success and retention may be achieved if remedial and developmental educators also address nonacademic and personal factors related to student success by providing clear student guidelines, integrating first-year transition into course work, using intrusive academic advising to treat the nonacademic and personal factors, and offering traditional developmental education course work and tutoring to address academic factors (Fowler & Boylan, 2010). According to the study results, a structured developmental education program that identifies, focuses on, and addresses students' academic, nonacademic, and personal factors can positively affect student success and retention.

VALUE ADDED AT MORGAN STATE UNIVERSITY

My first book, What Works at Historically Black Colleges and Universities (HBCUs): Nine Strategies for Increasing Retention and Graduation Rates, *was published in 2016. In the book, I identify nine strategies for enhancing student success: (1) leadership, (2) branding, (3) data mining, (4) frontloading, (5) case management, (6) strategic initiatives, (7) leveraging external resources, (8) technology, and (9) networking. Since I submitted my manu-*

script to my publisher in 2015, Morgan has continued its efforts to increase retention and foster completion.

One successful strategy to increase retention and graduation rates has been improving first-year advising. In collaboration with the Center for Academic Success and Achievement (CASA), the Office of Student Success and Retention (OSSR) at Morgan has utilized Starfish Retention Solutions by Hobsons, an early-alert, advising, and connection tool to support student academic success and retention, to assist with the academic advising of all first-year freshmen, who are advised by CASA and OSSR staff. Departmental liaisons have been identified to provide additional curriculum details and advising strategies for the CASA and OSSR staff. Holds are placed on first-year students' accounts, preventing them from making changes to their course schedules without consulting with an academic adviser first.

Once first-year students have earned at least 24 credits with a 2.0 minimum cumulative GPA and have declared a major, they are reassigned to their departmental or faculty adviser for the balance of their matriculation. All of the notes from first-year advising meetings are saved in Starfish for faculty advisors to refer to in subsequent advising meetings.

Every student has an online advising folder through Starfish. We now have more than 350,000 unique data points in Starfish since its adoption in January 2014. Annual analysis of Starfish by the Office of Institutional Research at Morgan finds a correlation between Starfish and midterm and final grades that can be observed in both positive and negative directions: With Starfish alerts, grades are likely to improve from midterm to final, and without Starfish alerts, grades may slip from midterm to final.

For the OSSR advising and counseling staff, Starfish, Degree Works, and Education Advisory Board Student Success Collaborative (EAB SSC) have greatly reduced the hours spent identifying cohorts of students to be contacted manually. EAB SSC is a three-pronged integrative approach to address student success through technology, research, and consulting. The first prong, SSC-Campus, is a comprehensive student analytics and support-technology platform that integrates analytics, interaction, and workflow tools. SSC-Campus has expanded OSSR advisers' access to individual and collective academic-performance data, facilitated communication among academic advisers and academic-support offices, and generated institutional reports in real time. By identifying and exploring factors that have the potential to positively inform curriculum, academic support, academic policy, and administrative-process decisions, this tool has significantly improved our capacity to retain and graduate our students.

Starfish has also allowed for continuous intervention by the OSSR staff for identified cohorts of students, especially the early alerts triggered by instructional faculty. The result has been automated, individualized e-mails and messages to students from OSSR staff. For students, Starfish has pro-

vided access to one online resource where all academic coaching and mentoring initiated by OSSR staff, academic advisers, and faculty can be obtained and acted on. Students' response rates to interventions, including the scheduling of appointments, have increased and facilitated more engagement with faculty, staff, and student-support offices. Integrating the Degree Works and EAB SSC tools into the existing Starfish initiative at Morgan has provided synergy and a "360-degree" approach to student success-innovation.

Together, Starfish Retention Solutions, Degree Works, and EAB SSC provide a seamless strategy to support students throughout their enrollment to include education planning, counseling and coaching, and targeting risk and intervention. Membership in EAB SSC has allowed Morgan more effectively to use institutional data and comprehensive analytics to assess students' academic progress, predict potential challenges, and develop highly targeted strategies that support their success.

Especially noteworthy is the utilization of the EAB SSC, Starfish, and Degree Works platforms by the entire university community, including professional and faculty advisers, provost, deans, department chairs, enrollment management, student-support offices, student affairs, institutional research, and assessment staff. A deficit model is not used at Morgan; we continually aim to provide invaluable, comprehensive, and transformative advising, tracking, and monitoring of all students, from matriculation to graduation.

ADDING VALUE AT GEORGIA STATE UNIVERSITY

Georgia State University, an urban public research university and minority-serving institution in Atlanta, has raised its six-year graduation rate from 32 percent in 2003 to more than 54 percent in 2017 through a combination of strategies, including predictive analytics; professional academic advisers who track more than 800 risk factors daily; and such innovations as in-class tutors, restructured gateway courses, and freshmen learning communities (McMurtrie, 2018). Georgia State's student population is 60 percent non-white, one-third first-generation, and 58 percent low-income or Pell-eligible. Despite the fact that these student populations graduate from college at lower rates, Georgia State today graduates more African American students than any other university in the country, and black students earn degrees at the same rate as whites (Herzog, 2018).

GSU has used predictive analytics to identify and monitor 800 risk factors for each of its 50,000 students on a continuous basis, which has resulted in dozens of Georgia State advisers holding more than 200,000 meetings with at-risk students during the past five years, ultimately leading to students to visit campus tutoring centers and instructors for remedial help and other academic-support services (Dimeo, 2017).

GSU administrators discovered that a grade of C earned in any entry-level course led to high dropout rates. Also, they found that students were switching their majors at a rate of 2.6 times before graduating. GSU created learning communities around metamajors, such as education, business, and STEM, so that students would be ready both academically and socially to select a major in their sophomore years while still staying on track in their entry-level and general-education courses (Kowalski, 2017). Georgia State removed unintended academic barriers, made pathways to graduation clearer, and invested in professional advisers, while providing students with the information that they need to be successful in a timely fashion (McMurtrie, 2018).

Georgia State University administrators have learned many lessons over the past 15 years of their transformation; one such lesson is that small amounts of money can yield major dividends for student success. For example, Georgia State has used microgrants called Panther Retention Grants to help students whose financial aid and loans don't close the gap for the payment of their tuition fees. Students do not have to apply for this funding; GSU administrators use predictive analytics and financial indicators to identify students with unmet financial need who are persisting and expected to graduate to award them with minigrants averaging $900 per semester (Kowalski, 2017). Providing a modest sum of money to students in good academic standing, many of whom are juniors or seniors, at the right time has proven effective for increasing retention and fostering degree completion at Georgia State University.

THE BOTTOM LINE

More than 50 years of higher-education research and practice have led to the establishment of proven strategies and best practices to enhance student success and increase graduation rates. These strategies and best practices include but are not limited to student–faculty engagement, academic advising, peer tutoring, active learning, first-year seminars or experiences, learning communities, mentoring and coaching, undergraduate research, internships, service learning, microgrants, flipped classrooms, financial assistance, predictive analytics, early warnings and alerts, developmental education, and reenrolling stopouts. It is in the best interests of postsecondary institutions to conduct self-assessments of current policies and practices and then develop programs and initiatives to address student-attrition issues of particular concern at the institution.

REFERENCES

Anderson, L. (2017, September). *State innovations for near-completers: Promising practices.* Denver, CO: Education Commission of the States. Retrieved from https://www.ecs.org/wp-content/uploads/State_Innovations-for-Near-Completers.pdf.

Attewell, P., Lavin, D., Domina, T., & Levey, T. (2006). New evidence on college remediation. *Journal of Higher Education, 77*(5), 886–924.

Borray, A. (2017, April 26). Predicting student success with big data. *Educause Review.* Retrieved from https://er.educause.edu/blogs/2017/4/predicting-student-success-with-big-data.

Brownell, J. E., & Swaner, L. E. (2009). High-impact practices: Applying the learning outcomes literature to the development of successful campus programs. *Peer Review, 11*(2), 26.

Chickering, A. W., & Ehrmann, S. C. (1996). Implementing the seven principles: Technology as lever. *AAHE Bulletin, 49*, 3–6.

Chickering, A. W., & Gamson, Z. F. (1987). Seven principles for good practice in undergraduate education. *AAHE Bulletin, 3*, 7.

Daniel, B. (2015). Big data and analytics in higher education: Opportunities and challenges. *British Journal of Educational Technology, 46*(5), 904–920.

Dimeo, J. (2017, July 19). Data dive. *Inside Higher Ed.* Retrieved from https://www.insidehighered.com/digital-learning/article/2017/07/19/georgia-state-improves-student-outcomes-data.

Ekowo, M., & Palmer, I. (2017, March). *Predictive analytics in higher education: Five guiding practices for ethical use.* Washington, DC: New America. Retrieved from https://www.newamerica.org/education-policy/policy-papers/predictive-analytics-higher-education/.

Fowler, P. R., & Boylan, H. R. (2010). Increasing student success and retention: A multidimensional approach. *Journal of Developmental Education, 34*(2), 2.

Herzog, K. (2018, January 16). How UWM peer Georgia State figured out how to graduate more black students. *Milwaukee Journal Sentinel.*

Kilgo, C. A., Sheets, J. K. E., & Pascarella, E. T. (2015). The link between high-impact practices and student learning: Some longitudinal evidence. *Higher Education, 69*(4), 509–525.

Kowalski, A. (2017, November 3). How Georgia State dramatically changed its graduation rate (and how other universities can, too). *Education Writers Association.* Retrieved from https://www.ewa.org/blog-higher-ed-beat/how-georgia-state-dramatically-changed-its-graduation-rate-and-how-other.

Kuh, G. D. (2008). *High-impact educational practices: What they are, who has access to them, and why they matter.* Washington, DC: Association of American Colleges and Universities.

Libassi, C. J. (2018, May 23). The neglected college race gap: Racial disparities among college completers. *Center for American Progress.* Retrieved from https://www.americanprogress.org/issues/education-postsecondary/reports/2018/05/23/451186/neglected-college-race-gap-racial-disparities-among-college-completers/.

McMurtrie, B. (2018, May 25). Georgia State U. made its graduation rate jump. How? *Chronicle of Higher Education.* Retrieved from https://www.chronicle.com/article/Georgia-State-U-Made-Its/243514?cid=wsinglestory_6_1a.

McNeal, M. (2016, December 15). Can financial advisors help more students graduate? One university thinks so. *EdSurge.* Retrieved from https://www.edsurge.com/news/2016-12-15-can-financial-advisors-help-more-students-graduate-one-university-thinks-so.

Nichols, A. H., Eberle-Sudré, K., & Welch, M. (Eds.). (2016, March). *Rising tide II: Do black students benefit as grad rates increase?* Washington, DC: Education Trust. Retrieved from https://files.eric.ed.gov/fulltext/ED566672.pdf.

Seemiller, C., & Grace, M. (2016). *Generation Z goes to college.* San Francisco: Jossey-Bass.

Shulock, N., & Moore, C. (2014, July). *State policy leadership in higher education: Six case studies.* Sacramento, CA: Sacramento State, Institute for Higher Education Leadership & Policy. Retrieved from https://files.eric.ed.gov/fulltext/ED574483.pdf.

Tinto, V. (2004, July). *Student retention and graduation: Facing the truth, living with the consequences* (Occasional paper 1). Washington, DC: Pell Institute for the Study of Opportunity in Higher Education. Retrieved from https://files.eric.ed.gov/fulltext/ED519709.pdf.

Tinto, V. (2006). Research and practice of student retention: What next? *Journal of College Student Retention: Research, Theory & Practice, 8*(1), 1–19.

Tucker, G. C. (2014). First generation. *Diverse Issues in Higher Education,* 24.

Turner, P., & Thompson, E. (2014). College retention initiatives meeting the needs of millennial freshman students. *College Student Journal, 48*(1), 94–104.

Ward, L., Siegel, M. J., & Davenport, Z. (2012). *First-generation college students: Understanding and improving the experience from recruitment to commencement.* San Francisco: Jossey-Bass.

Zatynski, M. (2016, March). No one strategy for success, but rather, a continuous line of support. In A. H. Nichols, K. Eberle-Sudré, & M. Welch (Eds.), *Rising tide II: Do black students benefit as grad rates increase?* Washington, DC: Education Trust. Retrieved from https://files.eric.ed.gov/fulltext/ED566672.pdf.

Chapter Ten

What's Next

Changing the Paradigm

As higher-education professionals continue to advocate for new and improved college retention and graduation measures, a new paradigm to promote college completion is emerging, an inclusive model that merges conventional practices and supports for students with nontraditional collaborations and advocacy from public and private partners, alumni, and successful noncompleters.

Tinto (2006) observes, that while many institutions tout the importance of increasing student retention, not enough had taken student retention seriously to the point that they were willing to commit needed resources and address the deeper structural issues that ultimately shape student persistence; many institutions are willing to append retention efforts to their ongoing activities but are much less willing to alter those activities in ways that address the deeper roots of student attrition. Tinto deduces that the really difficult work of shaping institutional practice, which requires postsecondary institutions to join forces with larger educational movements that seek to restructure higher education for all students, especially for low-income students, has yet to be tackled.

TRADITIONAL YET FUNDAMENTAL APPROACHES

Findings from a 2004 ACT study have significant implications for designing effective retention programs. Although many programs rely on traditional academic factors to identify students at risk of dropping out, this approach may be limited and may miss students who are at risk due to other, nonacademic factors. According to authors Lotkowski, Robbins, and Noeth (2004), students who master course content but fail to develop adequate academic self-confidence, academic goals, institutional commitment, and social support and involvement may still be at risk of dropping out of college. Therefore, they recommend that colleges and universities:

1. Determine their student characteristics and needs, set priorities among these areas of need, identify available resources, evaluate a variety of successful programs, and implement a formal, comprehensive retention program that best meets their institutional needs.
2. Take an integrated approach in their retention efforts that incorporates both academic and nonacademic factors into the design and development of programs to create a socially inclusive and supportive academic environment that addresses the social, emotional, and academic needs of students.
3. Implement an early-alert, assessment, and monitoring system based on HSGPA, ACT assessment scores, course-placement tests, first-semester college GPA, socioeconomic information, attendance records, and nonacademic information derived from formal college surveys and college student inventories to identify and build comprehensive profiles of students at risk of dropping out.
4. Determine the economic impact of their-college retention programs and their time to degree completion rates through a cost-benefit analysis of student dropout, persistence, assessment procedures, and intervention strategies to enable informed decision making with respect to types of interventions required—academic and nonacademic, including remediation and financial support.

While the most successful retention strategies often use an early-alert, assessment, and monitoring system based on academic factors, the ACT study suggests that retention efforts must be collaborative and coordinated, involving the entire academic community to ensure that student progress is actively monitored, resources are efficiently allocated, and programs are meeting their desired goals (Lotkowski, Robbins, & Noeth, 2004). The creation of a caring, supportive, and welcoming environment within the university through the development of positive student–faculty relationships, the presence of a well-resourced counseling center, and the encouragement of diversity is crucial for creating a sense of belonging (O'Keeffe, 2013). Even though O'Keeffe cites key factors for students at risk of noncompletion, such as mental health issues, disability, socioeconomic status, and ethnicity, the capacity of a student to develop a sense of belonging within the higher-education institution is recognized as being a crucial factor in determining student retention.

FACULTY'S ROLE IN THE VALUE PARADIGM

Two areas that are ripe for exploration in a new student-success paradigm are the effects of classroom practice on student learning and persistence and the impact of institutional investment in faculty- and staff-development programs on those outcomes (Tinto, 2006). Regarding faculty and staff development, Tinto stresses how increasingly clear it is that faculty actions, especially in the classroom, are crucial to institutional efforts to increase student retention. For example, Morales's 2014 qualitative study of academic resilience and the retention of low socioeconomic status students outlines successful strategies that faculty can adopt to increase the degree of resilience and persistence among first-generation college students:

- In designing their syllabi, faculty can begin their semesters with relatively straightforward and clear assignments that lend themselves to direct correlation between effort and outcome.
- While addressing students, faculty can talk about and promote previous students who have worked hard and succeeded, as well as how these students managed to do so.
- Building on these notions, professors who describe their own struggles with, and ultimate mastery of, their academic disciplines are particularly impactful.
- Another commonly reported characteristic of professors who helped encourage self-efficacy in their students is that they provided frequent, specific, and detailed feedback on as many assignments as possible, especially early in the semester.
- Another faculty approach that appears to bolster self-efficacy is the provision of choice when it came to course assignments. Many students expressed a sense of empowerment when they worked on an assignment or topic that they chose.
- Faculty can enhance self-efficacy by emphasizing the developmental and nonlinear nature of academic competence and achievement, helping students learn from their "failures" by stressing learning as a growth process rather than an "either you have it or you don't" construct.
- Faculty can help students realistically appraise their own strengths and weaknesses by giving ungraded pretests; having individual, private conferences to discuss results; and helping students uncover areas for improvement without the stress and emotions tied to grades and evaluation.
- Another strategy for faculty to implement is to take time to discuss the students' previous schooling experiences, specifically the quality and rigor of their precollege education.

- Faculty members and advisers can work with students to jointly identify skills, attributes, and competencies that they need in order to be successful and meet their academic and professional goals.
- Faculty should encourage more students to seek out and take advantage of available assistance through campus resources, such as writing centers and labs; continuous integration of resources can eventually engender and encourage help-seeking tendencies and the procurement of invaluable protective factors.
- Faculty can create assignments or activities that require students to attend university events or interact with available resources.
- Faculty should continually offer themselves as a resource, inviting students to visit them during office hours and offering letters of recommendation.
- Faculty can bring the work world into their classrooms to make future employment a more realistic and tangible entity by bringing in speakers from career fields related to their academic disciplines; creating assignments where students explore concepts inherent to prospective careers; facilitating and promoting available internships, employment opportunities, and graduate assistantships; and pointing out the value of early and constant résumé building.

While Morales states that it is unrealistic to expect all faculty to engage in all of the practices outlined here, what can be enacted depends on the academic discipline, the level of the students (freshmen, sophomores, etc.), the personality and expertise of the faculty member, and the mission of the institution. Morales asserts that, if a majority of faculty at a given institution operate in ways that promote and facilitate the resilience tenets described, then the overall climate and culture of the institution will foster greater success for the students who are often the most vulnerable and least likely to succeed. Tinto (2006) supposes:

> It is also the case that most institutions do not align their reward systems to the goal of enhanced student retention. It is one thing to talk about the importance of increasing student retention, it is another to invest scarce resources and adopt institutional faculty and staff reward systems that promote the behaviors that would reinforce that goal. It is little wonder then that while many faculty are willing to publicly proclaim the importance of retaining each and every student, they are in private the first to argue, on university campuses at least, that they will not get promoted and tenured unless they get research grants and publish. Unless the education and retention of students is not rewarded, in particular through promotion and tenure systems, many faculty will only give it lip service. (p. 9)

Faculty members at Georgia State University (GSU) did not initially embrace administrators' ambitious efforts to increase retention and graduation rates. GSU faculty were concerned that either predictive analytics would be used to label students and limit their opportunities or that predictive data would have a "big brother" effect, exercising too much control over students (Dimeo, 2017). Some faculty feared that some students would be steered toward easier majors; however, since GSU began providing advisers with information about job prospects and starting salaries for many industries, as well as students' financial aid packages, the university's two fastest-growing majors are computer science and biology.

Georgia State partnered with its faculty to "flip" more than 8,000 seats, mostly in introductory courses, using adaptive-learning technology (McMurtrie, 2018). With plans to flip an additional 12,000 to 15,000 seats over the next three years, traditional lecture sections are being replaced with students reviewing new material on their own and applying the concepts, with personalized in-class attention.

THE IMPORTANCE OF MINORITY-SERVING INSTITUTIONS (MSIs)

According to a new report by the American Council on Education (ACE), lower-income students who attend minority-serving colleges are more likely to improve their economic status than are those who attend other postsecondary institutions (Espinosa, Kelchen, & Taylor, 2018). The ACE report finds that income mobility was two to three times higher at minority-serving institutions than at non-minority-serving colleges and universities. The ACE study's mobility rate was calculated by taking the proportion of an institution's students who came from families in the bottom quintile of the income distribution (lowest-income students) and multiplying that by the proportion of these lowest-income students who, by age 30, moved to the top quintile of the income distribution. At a time when many MSIs are struggling with low general and educational expenditures and endowment sizes, the outsized performance of MSIs in generating income mobility as evidenced in the 2018 ACE report, even while they are operating with limited resources, makes a strong case for increased investment in these institutions.

MSIs serve the nation by educating the country's most vulnerable students, including minority, first-generation, and low-income students, while operating on relatively limited budgets. The ACE study findings undergird long-held beliefs by proponents of MSIs that they are poised to meet the widespread demand for higher education by minority, low-income, and first-generation students (Fain, 2018b).

The ACE report asserts the value of MSIs as a "viable path up the economic ladder for millions of students and reinforces the value proposition of higher education as a path to greater prosperity for individuals, families, and whole communities" (Espinosa, Kelchen, & Taylor, 2018). As policy makers develop metrics at the state and federal levels, policies that go beyond enrollment, retention, completion, debt, and repayment rates and include such measures as economic mobility should not be overlooked.

POLITICS AND POLICY IN THE NEW PARADIGM

Findings of a 2006 study of the determinants of college graduation rates at public and private colleges in the United States strongly suggest that the evaluation of public colleges based on raw graduation rates is inappropriate. Additionally, the report recommends that an assessment of institutions' graduation rates be adjusted to account for the diverse financial and student inputs to colleges. This finding presents a more optimistic portrayal of public-sector performance than is generally assumed by focusing attention on how graduation rates in the two sectors are related in different ways to various institutional characteristics (Scott, Bailey, & Kienzl, 2006). Beyond just monitoring institutional performance through a new federal tracking system that should be sensitive to the diversity of institutions and institutional missions, Tinto (2004) suggests there are a number of actions the federal government can take to promote innovation:

- Greatly expand such programs as the Fund for the Improvement of Postsecondary Education (FIPSE), which provides institutions resources to develop and pilot innovative programs to improve student persistence and graduation over time, particularly for low-income and first-generation students.
- Because college preparation matters, especially for first-generation and low-income students, create a special national initiative to address the retention of underprepared college students, where colleges and universities, working with high schools, can do more not only in linking their efforts but also in being more innovative in the use of summer-bridge and first-year developmental education programs.
- Provide support for state demonstration programs that would encourage states to "think outside the box"; while some states have established statewide efforts to improve retention, there is more that can and should be done.
- Join with other organizations to support the development of programs within universities that enable future faculty to acquire the skills needed to teach at the postsecondary level.

- The federal government can enhance transfer programs by conducting a careful assessment and dissemination of best transfer practices, in particular in those institutions, both rural and urban, that serve low-income students, and by providing funds to develop effective transfer programs, especially for those institutions serving low-income students.
- The federal government should remove disincentives that discourage institutions from serving low-income and first-generation students, such as how loan default rates are calculated for each institution of higher education.
- Increase student aid to address the financial barriers that low-income students face by substantially increasing Pell Grant funding and by encouraging states and institutions to link increases in need-based aid to increases in college tuition.
- The federal government should expand funding for TRIO, which includes eight programs targeted to serve and assist low-income individuals, first-generation college students, and individuals with disabilities to progress through the academic pipeline from middle school to postbaccalaureate programs.

In 2017, 35 states had a formula or policy in place to allocate a portion of funding based on such performance indicators as course completion, time to degree, transfer rates, the number of degrees awarded, and the number of low-income and minority graduates. A 2011 study provides evidence that for one state, Tennessee, public institutions did not respond to the monetary incentives created by the state of Tennessee's adoption of performance-funding policies (Sanford & Hunter, 2011).

For example, Sanford and Hunter find that the introduction of retention and six-year graduation rates as a measure included in performance-funding in 1997 did not result in a statistically significant difference in the mean retention or six-year graduation rates at Tennessee institutions compared to their peers. Additionally, the doubling of the monetary incentive associated with the retention and six-year graduation-rate measures by the state in 2005 was not associated with increases in retention rates at Tennessee institutions compared to their peer institutions.

The results of Sanford and Hunter's study suggest that states' adoption of performance-funding programs, such as the one in Tennessee, may not incentivize the change in institutional outcomes as desired by state leaders at their current funding levels. Sanford and Hunter recommend that policy makers (1) consider increasing the financial incentives tied to these policies in order to elicit their desired change in institutional outcomes, or (2) consider other methods to improve institutional outcomes. A 2014 study of Pennsylvania's State System of Higher Education performance-based-funding model suggests that degree completions within the state had not systematically increased and further concludes that performance-based funding is an ineffective model in terms of its ability to increase college completion (Hillman, Tandberg, & Gross, 2014).

Two 2017 studies add to a growing body of research that indicates that performance-based-funding policies may not work or have unintended consequences, with some of those problems being linked to design flaws (Fain, 2017). One study exposes equity problems with performance funding, where minority-serving institutions in states with performance-funding formulas lost significant funding on a per-student basis compared with other colleges in those states or with minority-serving institutions in states without performance funding, thereby jeopardizing the missions of these institutions (Hillman & Corral, 2017).

FINANCING POSTSECONDARY EDUCATION: WHO SHOULD PAY?

Some research provides evidence of a positive association between state funding and college-graduation rates; specifically, when other factors are held constant, a 10 percent increase in state appropriations per full-time-equivalent (FTE) student at four-year public institutions is associated with approximately a 0.64 percent increase in graduation rates (Zhang, 2009). This positive link appears to hold for both institutions that have enjoyed an increase in state funding and those that have experienced a reduction.

Zhang's study makes it clear that it is mainly the state appropriations that have a positive impact on graduation rates, a result consistent with the perspective of resource dependence, which holds that internal organizational activities are influenced primarily by the actions of external resource providers. Zhang acquiesces that a decline in state appropriation, when other factors are held constant, would most likely lead to a reduction in instructional expenditures, a reduction unlikely to be remedied through internal resource reallocation.

Since the start of the Great Recession in 2007, most states have cut higher-education funding deeply, in part the result of a revenue collapse caused by the economic downturn but also a result of misguided policy choices (Mitchell, Palacios, & Leachman, 2014). While state policy makers have relied overwhelmingly on spending cuts to make up for lost revenues, the subsequent cost shifts harm students and families, especially those with low incomes.

Mitchell, Palacios, and Leachman chart the following consequences of reductions in state funding to higher education: (1) Students are taking on more debt; (2) tuition costs are deterring some students from enrolling in college; (3) tuition increases are likely deterring low-income students, in particular, from enrolling; and (4) tuition increases may be pushing lower-income students toward less-selective institutions, reducing their future earnings. Many public colleges have both increased tuition and reduced spending in an attempt to compensate for lost state funding, potentially compromising the quality of the education and jeopardizing student outcomes. Mitchell, Palacios, and Leachman call for the urgent renewal of investments in higher education to promote college affordability and quality.

A 2016 randomized experiment used to estimate the impact of a private need-based-grant program on college persistence and degree completion among students from low-income families attending 13 public universities across Wisconsin indicates that offering students additional grant aid increases the odds of bachelor's degree attainment over four years, thereby helping to diminish income inequality in higher education (Goldrick-Rab, Kelchen, Harris, & Benson, 2016). The authors resolve the following in their discussion of the experiment:

> While the effectiveness of financial aid is often assessed in terms of college attendance, higher education's ability to affect social mobility hinges in part on students from low-income families completing college degrees. This study provides new experimental evidence indicating that increasing need-based grant aid is an effective approach for inducing current students to remain enrolled in college, earn slightly more credits, and get somewhat better grades, contributing to improved rates of on-time (four-year) bachelor's degree completion. Moreover, grant aid contributes to the attenuation of inequality in college graduation. (Goldrick-Rab, Kelchen, Harris, & Benson, 2016, p. 1801)

MORGAN STATE UNIVERSITY: GLASS HALF-FULL

Beginning with the fall 2010 freshmen cohort, Morgan has achieved retention rates above 70 percent for seven consecutive years. This was achieved through a combination of early-intervention strategies, systematic tracking and monitoring, and academic coaching and mentoring. The Office of Student Success and Retention (OSSR) staff spend most of their time monitoring and tracking students' finances and satisfactory academic progress. The OSSR works to produce graduates of Morgan State University who are well prepared to meet the challenges of an internship, graduate school, professional school, and career following their successful matriculation and graduation from the institution. As a result of grants from the Lumina Foundation, the Bill & Melinda Gates Foundation, and the Maryland Higher Education Commission, Morgan has invested in new technologies, including the Education Advisory Board's (EAB) Student Success Collaborative (SSC), Hobson's Starfish Retention Solutions, and Ellucian's Degree Works.

These tools have assisted the OSSR with strategic tracking and monitoring, auditing and degree planning, academic coaching and mentoring, course redesign, and predictive analytics. Our intrusive, intentional student-success initiatives have helped Morgan gain national recognition, winning the 2017 Hobsons Education Advances Award for Student Success and Advisement, the Association of Public and Land-Grant Universities' (APLU) 2016 Turning Points Award, and the 2015 APLU Project Degree Completion Award for our outstanding efforts to increase retention rates and promote student success; Morgan State University is the only historically black college or university (HBCU) to ever have won these national awards.

In 2016, in an effort to enhance and sustain increases in retention in graduation rates, Morgan's president, Dr. David Wilson, hosted a "deep dive" retreat for his cabinet, deans, chairs, and senior administrators. Dr. Timothy Renick, vice provost and vice president for enrollment management and student success at Georgia State University (GSU), presented in person an exciting example of strategic, systemic, and evidence-based change at GSU that set the tone for the introduction of a proposal for a new strategic campaign to increase Morgan State University's graduation rates.

The Morgan State University "50 by 25" Initiative: Getting More Students across the Finish Line, a campaign to increase Morgan's graduation rate to 50 percent by 2025, has continued into its third year, with emphasis on three central themes: (1) advising and degree planning, (2) faculty development and course redesign, and (3) beyond financial aid (BFA). The "50 by 25" campaign includes half-day, check-in meetings twice per year, in April and November, for the cabinet, deans, chairs, and senior administrators to report on their progress. The adoption of Starfish, Degree Works, and EAB SSC support the "50 by 25" campaign to continue gains in student success.

Even with 10 percent increases in both retention and graduation rates at Morgan, we continue to press forward to meet our goal of a 50 percent graduation rate by 2025. Second-to-third-, third-to-fourth-, and fourth-to-fifth-year retention rates continue to show improvements as we implement our "value-added" student-success strategies. The fifth-year graduation rate for the 2013 cohort of freshmen is already higher than the six-year graduation rate for the 2012 cohort of freshmen. Morgan is poised to exceed its 50 by 25 goal and set a new standard for student success at HBCUs.

A 50 percent graduation rate at Morgan State University represents an overperformance of 20 percentage points; based on students' household-income quartile and/or first-generation status and/or race and ethnicity, Morgan's projected graduation rate is about 30 percent. Focusing on our strengths instead of our weaknesses, building on our wins, adopting technologies to streamline student support, and fostering visionary leadership that supports innovation and creativity are what keep our glass more toward full and less toward empty at Morgan State University.

PARTNERS IN THE PARADIGM

The focus of a 2018 doctoral dissertation is how two prominent foundations, the Bill & Melinda Gates Foundation and the Lumina Foundation, identify problems, develop potential solutions, and attempt to foster their adoption across states and higher-education institutions (Lahr, 2018). These foundations participate in policy-learning processes, whereby they modify strategies based on new information, input from partner organizations, and past investments in order to serve as influential political actors within the higher-education completion agenda. As these foundations raise awareness of their goals, problem definitions, and solutions and take an active role in seeking out support for their higher-education agendas, affecting both state policy and higher-education institutions, they are crucial allies in the new paradigm for postsecondary education.

After 18 years of focus on college completion, the Lumina Foundation has added racial justice and equity as a priority. It announced in June 2018 that 19 colleges and universities will receive grant awards totaling $625,000 from its Fund for Racial Justice and Equity, a project of Rockefeller Philanthropy Advisors (Whitford, 2018). The new grants were established with the goal of improving race relations on college campuses. With an endowment in excess of $1 billion, Lumina Foundation is the nation's largest private foundation focused solely on increasing Americans' success in higher education. Through grants for research, innovation, communication, and evaluation, as well as policy education and leadership development, Lumina Foundation addresses issues that affect access and educational attainment among all students, particularly underserved student groups.

The Bill & Melinda Gates Foundation works with educators, researchers, technologists, foundations, policy makers, and other partners to help public colleges and universities affordably and efficiently guide more low-income students to degree completion. The foundation works with partners to transform higher-education models for colleges and universities so that more students, especially low-income and first-generation students, graduate at higher rates, with high-quality degrees or certificates at an affordable price.

In 2018, the Association of Public and Land-Grant Universities (APLU) announced that a group of 100 public universities, organized in 10 "transformation clusters" formed around universities with common priorities, will work to produce hundreds of thousands of additional degrees while also reducing achievement gaps for underrepresented student groups (Fain, 2018a). The new transformation clusters resemble the University Innovation Alliance (UIA), a coalition of 11 large public research universities that work together on improving graduation rates, also with a focus on lower-income and underrepresented students.

In addition to the new APLU project, the American Association of State Colleges and Universities (AASCU) has created a coalition of 44 member institutions that are working on a student-success project focused on reimagining the first year of college. The Frontier Set is a group of 30 colleges and universities, state systems, and supporting organizations working to improve student access and success. The APLU, UIA, and AASCU initiatives are all funded by the Bill & Melinda Gates Foundation.

THE BOTTOM LINE

Postsecondary education's value paradigm must involve evolution; the institutions making the greatest strides in student success always are endeavoring to explore new strategies, expand existing initiatives, and engage with colleagues and leaders in the field of higher education. The value paradigm for postsecondary education ought to encompass faculty and changes to faculty policies and incentives; investment in MSIs and HBCUs; a proactive policy agenda at the federal and state levels; funding and resources to support institutions; student financial aid enhancements; technology and innovation; and partnerships with professional organizations, foundations, alumni, and noncompleters to collaborate and work as advocates on behalf of higher education. Now more than ever, postsecondary education offers an invaluable service to the nation's citizens—education and experience to prepare them to live their best lives.

REFERENCES

Dimeo, J. (2017, July 19). Data dive. *Inside Higher Ed.* Retrieved from https://www. insidehighered.com/digital-learning/article/2017/07/19/georgia-state-improves-student-outcomes-data.

Espinosa, L. L., Kelchen, R., & Taylor, M. (2018). *Minority serving institutions as engines of upward mobility.* Washington, DC: American Council on Education. Retrieved from https:// www.acenet.edu/news-room/Documents/MSIs-as-Engines-of-Upward-Mobility.pdf.

Fain, P. (2017, December 18). Negative findings on performance-based funding. *Inside Higher Ed.* Retrieved from https://www.insidehighered.com/quicktakes/2017/12/18/negative-findings-performance-based-funding.

Fain, P. (2018, February 21). Collaborating on completion. *Inside Higher Ed.* Retrieved from https://www.insidehighered.com/news/2018/02/21/public-universities-band-together-completion-rates-and-achievement-gaps.

Fain, P. (2018, June 13). The minority-serving-college mobility bump. *Inside Higher Ed.* Retrieved from https://www.insidehighered.com/news/2018/06/13/minority-serving-colleges-top-peers-economic-mobility-report-finds.

Goldrick-Rab, S., Kelchen, R., Harris, D. N., & Benson, J. (2016). Reducing income inequality in educational attainment: Experimental evidence on the impact of financial aid on college completion. *American Journal of Sociology, 121*(6), 1762–1817.

Hillman, N., & Corral, D. (2017). The equity implications of paying for performance in higher education. *American Behavioral Scientist, 61*(14), 1757–1772.

Hillman, N. W., Tandberg, D. A., & Gross, J. P. (2014). Performance funding in higher education: Do financial incentives impact college completions? *Journal of Higher Education, 85*(6), 826–857.

Lahr, H. E. (2018). Policymaking for college completion: How foundations develop their higher education agendas (Doctoral dissertation, Columbia University, 2018).

Lotkowski, V. A., Robbins, S. B., & Noeth, R. J. (2004). *The role of academic and non-academic factors in improving college retention* (ACT policy report). Iowa City: American College Testing.

McMurtrie, B. (2018, May 25). Georgia State U. made its graduation rate jump. How? *Chronicle of Higher Education*. Retrieved from https://www.chronicle.com/article/Georgia-State-U-Made-Its/243514?cid=wsinglestory_6_1a.

Mitchell, M., Palacios, V., & Leachman, M. (2014, May 1). *States are still funding higher education below prerecession levels*. Washington, DC: Center on Budget and Policy Priorities.

Morales, E. E. (2014). Learning from success: How original research on academic resilience informs what college faculty can do to increase the retention of low socioeconomic status students. *International Journal of Higher Education, 3*(3), 92.

O'Keeffe, P. (2013). A sense of belonging: Improving student retention. *College Student Journal, 47*(4), 605–613.

Sanford, T., & Hunter, J. M. (2011). Impact of performance-funding on retention and graduation rates. *Education Policy Analysis Archives/Archivos Analíticos de Políticas Educativas, 19*.

Scott, M., Bailey, T., & Kienzl, G. (2006). Relative success? Determinants of college graduation rates in public and private colleges in the US. *Research in Higher Education, 47*(3), 249–279.

Tinto, V. (2004, July). *Student retention and graduation: Facing the truth, living with the consequences* (Occasional paper 1). Washington, DC: Pell Institute for the Study of Opportunity in Higher Education. Retrieved from https://files.eric.ed.gov/fulltext/ED519709.pdf.

Tinto, V. (2006). Research and practice of student retention: What next? *Journal of College Student Retention: Research, Theory & Practice, 8*(1), 1–19.

Whitford, E. (2018, June 19). Moving beyond college completion. *Inside Higher Ed*. Retrieved from https://www.insidehighered.com/news/2018/06/19/lumina-foundation-moves-beyond-college-completion-grants-improve-campus-racial.

Zhang, L. (2009). Does state funding affect graduation rates at public four-year colleges and universities? *Educational Policy, 23*(5), 714–731.

About the Author

Dr. Tiffany Beth Mfume is the assistant vice president (AVP) for student success and retention at Morgan State University and, as such, manages new-student and parent orientation, placement testing, Starfish Retention Solutions' Early Alert and Connect systems, first-year advisement, financial literacy, alumni mentoring, and academic recovery, among other programs and services. Dr. Mfume's leadership has helped to promote 10 percent increases in retention and graduation rates, from a 63 percent (2006 cohort) to a 73 percent (2015 cohort) retention rate in 2016 and from a 28 percent (2005 cohort) to a 38 percent (2011 cohort) graduation rate in 2017. Morgan's Office of Student Success and Retention (OSSR) was selected as a national winner of the 2017 Hobsons Education Advances Award for Student Success and Advisement, the 2016 Association of Public and Land-grant Universities (APLU) Turning Points: From Setback to Student Success Award, and the 2015 Association of Public and Land-Grant Universities (APLU) Project Degree Completion Award, which serves as evidence of the effective student-success model at Morgan State University. Morgan is the only HBCU to ever have won these national awards. Prior to her appointment as AVP, Dr. Mfume served for 15 years as director of the OSSR and three years as the coordinator of the ACCESS-SUCCESS program, a six-week summer-bridge program for freshmen at Morgan State University. Also, for two years, Dr. Mfume worked as an academic adviser for the Comprehensive Program for Undeclared Majors at Morgan State University. Prior to her employment history at Morgan State University, Dr. Mfume worked six years as program coordinator for the Society for In Vitro Biology, a nonprofit research association. Immediately following the completion of her undergraduate degree, Dr. Mfume went to work for Birch & Davis Associates in Washington, DC, as a management consultant and meeting planner. Dr. Mfume enjoys international travel with her husband, reading, and public speaking. Dr. Mfume is author of the nationally recognized book *What Works at Historically Black Colleges and Universities (HBCUs): Nine Strategies for Increasing Retention and Graduation Rates*, published in 2016 by Rowman & Littlefield.